D1094033

SHAKESPEARE *the Salesman*

SHAKESPEARE
The Salesman

BY
WILLIAM B. BURRUSS

42-13416

1942
THE DARTNELL CORPORATION
CHICAGO

FIRST PRINTING
November 1941

CONTENTS

WORLD'S BEST SALESMAN 13

CONFIDENCE 21

ENTHUSIASM—THE WILL TO WIN 26

OPEN-MINDEDNESS 32

HUMAN UNDERSTANDING 38

AN ALL-OUT EFFORT FOR SUCCESS 49

PERSISTENCE 49

ADAPTABILITY 50

FORCE 51

USE OF SUGGESTION 51

MAKING THE VOICE WORK FOR YOU 52

GOOD ETHICS AND CODE OF PROCEDURE 58

SALES TECHNIQUE 63

THE LAWS OF A SALE 71

BUYING MOTIVES 82

SINCERITY 91

FOOTNOTES 103

ABOUT BILL BURRUSS

By the Publisher

As YOU pick up this book you may wonder, as a friend of mine did a few days ago, if there is any need for another book on salesmanship. My friend asked me, "With all the books on salesmanship, isn't it just about impossible to say anything new on the subject?" My answer to him was that it is not always what you say, but how you say it, that counts. Of course, there are many books on salesmanship, and some of them seem all too similar to many others which have gone before. But every now and then comes a man who finds a way to dress old, tried, sound ideas in new clothes.

I am happy to report that this book is that kind of volume. Bill Burruss is a salesman who learned selling the hard way. He has been selling for many years. He was not guilty of writing a book about salesmanship either, for the material in this book grew out of his long experience as a salesman, as a teacher of salesmanship, and as a leader of salesmen.

As I just said, Bill Burruss did not sit down to write a book on selling. From time to time, when he was still selling he was called upon to talk to fellow salesmen about the fine art of persuading people to buy. Gradually he developed the idea that another "Bill" was the greatest salesman the world ever knew. That other "Bill" was William Shakespeare.

Every time Burruss talked to other salesmen about his friend William Shakespeare, these salesmen went out and told people about Bill's talk. There was such a demand for his talk on William Shakespeare that he finally had to start charging a fee.

Burruss has delivered the talk, "Shakespeare the Salesman," more than 1,100 times. He has been paid more than $100,000 for these talks. In many cities and before many organizations he has returned again and again for repeat engagements.

Once more I repeat, Bill Burruss learned selling the hard way. When, at the ripe old age of eleven years, he began selling subscriptions to the *Youth's Companion*, there were no books on salesmanship. Nor were there any books on salesmanship to read while he was selling "papers" of needles and pins in Carroll County, Missouri, where he was born.

Nor were there any books on salesmanship when he paid his way through seven years of university training, winning his A.B. and LL.B. degrees, while selling advertising and a wonderful book called *The Cottage Doctor*. This was one of those books which was supposed to tell you what to do before the doctor arrived. There was an old joke about the book which said that the doctor always had to hurry to a patient who owned one of the books, else the patient would be dead before the doctor arrived.

Bill Burruss had a good start in law practice, being a member of the staff of Ballinger, Ronald and Battle, of Seattle. Ballinger was the famed Secretary of the Interior under President William Howard Taft. But Burruss had started his career as a salesman, and I suppose the profession of law seemed tame to him.

Anyway he went back to Missouri and started a typewriter and sewing machine agency. Here he was treading a path trod by many a man who became famous in the sales field.

From sewing machines and typewriters Burruss went into insurance. From October 1906 to September 1907 he led the entire field force of the Provident Life and Trust Company, when he was made general agent for the company at Norfolk, Virginia, then transferred to Springfield, Missouri. From there he went to Kansas City as joint general agent of the company which had mutualized and changed its name to the Provident Mutual Life Insurance Company. Soon he was chairman of the Speakers' Committee of the Kansas City Chamber of Commerce, and once when he was paid $100 for substituting for former Senator James A. Reed of Missouri, he decided to give up insurance and devote all his time to teaching and organization work.

It was a fortunate decision—many of the country's most famous companies have called on Bill Burruss to train and organize salesmen. He has worked in every state in the Union and has spoken or worked with groups of salesmen in every city of more than 100,000 population in the United States, Canada, and Mexico.

J. C. ASPLEY

SHAKESPEARE
The Salesman

WORLD'S BEST SALESMAN

There is a tide in the affairs of men
Which taken at the flood leads on to fortune.[1]

The greatest and best salesman who ever lived was,
    Not a book agent.
    Nor a life insurance man.
    He didn't sell stocks and bonds.
    He wasn't a "knight of the road."
    He never rang a door bell.
    Nor canvassed from house to house.
    He presented no free gifts in order to get in.
    He carried no samples.
    He distributed no literature.
And yet he was the world's top salesman.

He was born and lived in a sleepy little village, on a sleepy little river, in sleepy old England. His name was William Shakespeare. He is known as the "Immortal Bard of Avon."

Why should this be of any interest to you?

You may be a salesman fighting for promotion, increased salary, or an additional commission check.

Or you may not consider yourself a salesman in any sense of the word—this in spite of the fact that since the world began salesmanship has always been present in every human relation.

When Eve, according to reliable reports, sold Adam the idea that he should eat the apple, that would not be considered by a great many people as a sale. But, whether

Footnote references begin on page 103

true or false, this sale has had tremendous effects on the lives and fortunes of those of us who have followed.

You may be a professional man, an engineer, a lawyer, a physician, a professor, a minister, or a funeral director;

You may be a bookkeeper, a plumber, a carpenter, or bricklayer;

You may be a cashier, telephone operator, hat check girl, or a clerk in an office;

You may be a housewife, a boy or a girl in school;

You may be a day laborer, a policeman, a fireman, a streetcar conductor, or a night watchman!

You may be repeating to yourself those old falsehoods:

"I am not a salesman.

"I don't sell anything.

"I could never make myself sell anything.

"I am not the type to be a salesman.

"Salesmen are born not made.

"You can't change human nature."

You may not think that you are interested in any way in the art of salesmanship. You may feel that in your work, in your daily relations with your friends, family, and relatives salesmanship plays no part. But that's merely your opinion at present. Now opinions change, but facts always remain the same.

Well, this is a fact.

You are a salesman.

Maybe a good one.

Perhaps only fair.

Or God forbid—a very poor one.

But you are a salesman in every contact you make—

In every human relationship,

In all of your doings with other human beings,

Even in your relationships with the animal kingdom.

Your manner, your personality, your ability to understand, will affect your happiness, your income, your position, your development, and your well-being.

And your ability as a salesman also affects everyone with whom you come in contact.

When two people meet, a sale takes place.

You sell them or they will sell you.

Sometimes it is a double sale. You sell each other.

Since salesmanship is an important part of your life, why not let the master salesman, William Shakespeare, show you how to be a good salesman?

Shakespeare was the greatest salesman who ever lived.

You may not agree with this statement. You may have an entirely different opinion.

Several years ago I was traveling on a special train carrying automobile dealers to the Stutz Convention at Indianapolis.

One of the Stutz dealers asked me if I knew Charles Schwab, the great steel man. I answered that I had never had the pleasure of being introduced to him.

The dealer said, "We pick up his private car at Harrisburg, Pennsylvania. He is a real fellow. I'll take you up and introduce you to him, if you would like to meet him."

We went up to his private car, and Mr. Schwab was very gracious. It was during prohibition, and I was delighted with the lemonade Mr. Schwab had his servant fix for me.

Mr. Schwab had been acclaimed for years as a great salesman.

As a conversationalist, Mr. Schwab had few equals. He turned to me with a twinkle in his eye and said:

"You're the chap that makes a talk on 'Shakespeare the Salesman,' aren't you?"

"Yes," I admitted. "I am."

"Well," he replied, "I don't agree with you. Shakespeare is a wonderful writer, but not a salesman. There are too many people nowadays making salesmen out of everybody. My own idea has been expressed by Emerson, or at least Elbert Hubbard attributes the expression to Ralph Waldo Emerson, although I must admit I never ran across it in any of Emerson's works. Now according to Hubbard, Emerson said:

" 'If you build a better mousetrap, the world will beat a path to your door, though it be in a wilderness.'

"What do you say to that?"

"Maybe you are right," I replied and changed the subject.

A little later, I returned to the subject by asking Mr. Schwab, who at that time practically controlled Stutz Motor Car Company of America, a question.

"You believe, do you not, Mr. Schwab, that the Stutz is a good car?"

"The very best," he replied.

"You believe then that it is well built, properly styled, performs well, is priced right, and is the equal of any car on the market in dollar value?"

"We'll have no quarrel on that score. I'll go you one better. I think it's absolutely the best car made and offers the public the best buy on the market. It has no equal."

"Then Mr. Schwab," I interposed, "how do you reconcile your advocacy of Emerson's statement with these facts? Your dealers on this train are crying their eyes out because, in spite of all the fine qualities and value of the Stutz car, in spite of the fact that you have built it 'well enough,' the public won't come to the dealers' beautiful showrooms on the main street and look at it."

"Well," said Mr. Schwab with a chuckle. "Maybe Emerson didn't say what Hubbard said he did. After all, facts have at times troubled Hubbard. And," he added, "maybe what you say about Shakespeare being a salesman is true."

"As a matter of record, both positions are right, Mr. Schwab.

"Years ago when production was very low and demand high, buyers would seek out the maker of a superior product, even in a wilderness. Today, with production high, makers of products have to find their prospects, and good salesmanship is necessary.

"After all you have a right to your opinion, but did you ever know any two people who had the same opinions about everything? If so, was not one of them a lame brain, a nit wit, a spineless jelly fish, or a hypocrite?"

> *Opinion's but a fool, that makes us scan*
> *The outward habit by the inward man.*[2]

Opinions *do* differ, while facts remain constant.

Even a man and wife have different opinions—even a man and wife who have a newly born baby boy in a crib.

Both may be sitting nearby. They may be looking at the baby, both in deep thought.

Are both thinking the same thing?

The wife is thinking, "What a darling little baby this is; how happy and proud I am that it is our baby boy. In a few weeks he'll be crawling on the floor—in a few months, taking his first baby step and lisping his first baby words. A little later he'll trudge off to school without responsibility. Then in college winning honors. Finally out in the great world sweeping everything before him. A phenomenon of success. Finally, yes finally, becoming President of the United States."

She turns to her husband and says gently, "John, darling, what are you thinking?"

John came to with a start, scratched his head, and replied, "Me, I was just wondering how the hell they could build a crib like that for $4.95."

Your opinion may be that Shakespeare was not a salesman.

You may admit that he was a wonderful writer and adapter of plays.

You may agree with me that he was a great philosopher —a man who thoroughly understood human nature, a dramatist, an actor, musician, and a poet.

But not a salesman.

Maybe we should stop a moment and, as Socrates says, "define our terms."

What is salesmanship? Do you agree with me that it is:

> The ability to paint a picture so one can see what you see?
>
> The art of making people want to do the things you want them to do?
>
> The ability to make men think?
>
> The ability to present ideas logically so they are accepted?
>
> The ability to make men feel as well as think?
>
> The ability to create confidence?
>
> The ability to make people like you?
>
> The ability to establish your sincerity and the fact that you are rendering unselfish service?
>
> The ability to make people act?

If you accept these definitions, you must accept the fact that Shakespeare was a salesman—a real go-getter.

Let me now submit overwhelming proof of this statement. Shakespeare wrote or adapted thirty-seven plays.

He introduced over one thousand characters—

No two alike,
All different,
Some good,
Some bad,
Some indifferent,
From brilliant to dumb,
From the noblest to the most unscrupulous.

His characters portrayed or discussed practically all subjects and sold ideas so well that wherever you find civilization you find the collected works of William Shakespeare.

He is quoted everywhere, wherever men gather—in the pulpit or in the lowest dives.

Men sometimes quote him and think they are quoting the Bible, or think it was original, when what they said was first said by Shakespeare.

"Yes, that's true," you say, "but how does that prove your statement?"

Just remember this, no one knows what any character of Shakespeare's really said. We only know what Shakespeare said they said. He *was* the one thousand characters. He thought for them. He spoke for them. He was not only a sales manager of one thousand salesmen, he was each and every one of those salesmen. So he was the salesman with all the ability and qualifications of the thousand whom he created.

Stop for just a moment and realize the difficulties of a sales manager of, let us say, ten men.

They're all selling the same product.

They work for the same company; they use the same

literature. They're following the barrage of advertising that has been laid down by their company.

Their market has been identified, their prospects located, their prospects' needs surveyed and analyzed.

Their sales manager has directed them on how to approach, when to approach, and what to say.

He knows that the job of directing salesmen is very difficult, because he realizes most salesmen are like grasshoppers—excellent on distance, but poor on direction.

Most of us can understand the difficulties of his job, and if he does a good job he is considered, by most people, a good sales manager and a super-salesman.

Shakespeare was a sales manager of a thousand salesmen.

They didn't work for the same company.

They didn't sell the same products.

They had no barrage to prepare the way.

They were not all equipped with proper qualifications to think and talk.

These two qualifications have set men apart from the rest of the animal kingdom since the world began: the ability to think and the ability to express their thoughts.

Shakespeare had to think for a thousand salesmen.

He had to talk for them.

No one knows what Shakespeare's characters really said. We only know what Shakespeare, thinking and speaking for them, said, so any statement from any one of his characters was thought of and expressed by Shakespeare.

I feel you now are beginning to realize that there is a possibility that Shakespeare might have been a salesman.

What are some of the qualities essential to successful selling?

Confidence.

Enthusiasm.

Open-mindedness.

Human understanding.

Good ethics.

Sincerity.

Shakespeare had them all, and he taught others how to acquire them.

CONFIDENCE

Our doubts are traitors,
And make us lose the good we oft might win
By fearing to attempt.[1]

Books have been written about how to acquire confidence.

Lectures have been delivered.

Courses of instruction have been given.

All of them have been, or could have been, based on Shakespeare's statement on confidence.

Our doubts are traitors,
And make us lose the good we oft might win
By fearing to attempt.[2]

How often have we failed to sell or gain our desire because of fear?

We were afraid to try.

We might possibly lose.

And we lost "by fearing to attempt."

As a small boy, I knocked at the door of a stranger.

I had a package of needles and pins to sell.

No one answered the door.

My knees began to tremble and to bump each other.

My stomach began a series of flip-flops.

My heart seemed to be moving up into my throat, and I seemed to be choking and somewhat short of breath.

I began to talk to myself.

"It's too early in the morning.

"Besides it's Monday, and women are busy washing on Monday.

"Besides it's a rainy day, and people are blue and don't want to buy things.

"Someone has been here before me and sold her a similar package.

"Besides I don't feel very well."

I turned and walked off the porch.

An old gentleman stopped me.

"Trying to sell something, Sonny?"

"Yes," I gasped.

"Kinder skeered, ain't you?"

"Yes," I whispered.

"Ever heerd what Bill Shakespeare said?"

"No," I mumbled.

"Well, Bill said, 'You will always lose a sale if you won't try.' And as I remember it, he said to ask yourself three questions when you knock on the door.

"Fust one, 'Where am I now?' and answer it."

" 'Outside.' "

"Second one, 'Where will I be if I go in and get kicked out?' "

" 'Outside, same as I am now. But then I'll know what the place looks like.' "

"Third, 'Where will I be if I go in and *don't* get kicked out?' "

" 'Inside—the only place I can make a sale.' "

"Besides, it's safer. More people are killed or hurt leaving a prospect's house and crossing a street than are hurt inside.

"Remember, Sonny, what Bill Shakespeare said: 'You can't lose by going in—but you're sure to lose if you don't.' "

I have a long list of things I know I have lost by fearing to attempt, but I also have some rather worth-while accomplishments due to this old gentleman's rather interesting exposition of William Shakespeare's quotation on confidence.

> *Our doubts are traitors,*
> *And make us lose the good we oft might win*
> *By fearing to attempt.*[3]

If more people would, after reading this, simply sit down and recognize the fact that all is possible with confidence and that practically nothing is possible without it! If only this will help make people decide, from now on, to build up their confidence so they could meet any proposition or any situation properly equipped and successfully cope with it!

There is a solution for every problem.

You have only to find it.

The person with confidence continually seeks the solution. The person without confidence is very apt to give up easily and offer an alibi for his failure.

In order to have a reservoir of confidence, it is first necessary that we have confidence in our country and our government.

We must believe in the form of government under which we operate. We must believe in its ability to solve problems which are beyond our ability to handle alone.

We must believe and have confidence in the system of government under which we live, realizing the fact that the government, which gives us an opportunity to work out our destiny according to the dictates of our conscience and our judgment with the least possible interference, is a government well worth supporting and preserving.

We must appreciate the fact that we have the privilege of free speech and freedom of choice of any occupation or profession that we choose to enter; that we have the right to use the money we make in our effort in any way we choose. We can spend it, we can invest it, we can give it away. That is a matter for us and for us alone to decide.

We must realize that the privilege to worship as we please has been given to us, but must, as our other privileges are, be guaranteed by someone, or else it will be taken from us.

That someone must of necessity be our government.

We must also realize that these privileges, which are guaranteed to us by our form of government, were not obtained without effort and sacrifice.

Throughout the ages men have fought and died for these blessed privileges. We must realize, too, that merely because they were given to us practically on a platter is no reason why we should not be ready and willing to make whatever sacrifices are necessary to defend them.

We mustn't expect someone else to do it for us. We must be willing to do it ourselves.

If we can establish our confidence in our government and its tenets, we are then better able to establish confidence in the organization or group by which we're employed. By building this confidence in our employers we automatically build confidence in the product or service they offer for sale.

We likewise build confidence in ourselves and in our own ability to fight our way through to success—confidence in our own ability to solve any problem that may face us, in our own ability to win the rewards we want for ourselves and those we love.

Such a feeling of confidence will give us a new outlook on life and a larger capacity for accomplishment.

Oh yes, Shakespeare was a better salesman than even he knew or could realize.

In order to make confidence work more effectively for us, it should be based on knowledge whenever possible. We may not be able to prove many of the things we believe by definite knowledge of the actual facts, and so, in those cases, confidence has to be based on faith.

But when we're dealing with business or social problems, it is best for us to be equipped with exact knowledge.

We should know our product or the service we have to sell.

The rock of knowledge is a firm foundation for confidence.

Confidence based on knowledge is firm as Gibraltar.

Know your product.

> *As gentle and as jocund as to jest*
> *Go I to fight: truth hath a quiet breast.*[4]

ENTHUSIASM—THE WILL TO WIN

I see you stand like greyhounds in the slips,
Straining upon the start.[1]

The ability to acquire self-starting habits and enthusiasm may be difficult. Reading Shakespeare will help
because Shakespeare had the divine spark of enthusiasm.

He had it in immeasurable quantities.

He transmitted it to his characters.

In spite of difficulties and legal bans, he wrote or
adapted thirty-seven plays and many poems. Many of
his characters bubble over with enthusiasm.

They are truly self-starters. They have the necessary
spark.

Petruchio, while waiting for Katharina, the Shrew, says
to himself:

I will attend her here,
And woo her with some spirit when she comes.
Say that she rail: why then I'll tell her plain
She sings as sweetly as a nightingale:
Say that she frown; I'll say she looks as clear
As morning roses newly wash'd with dew:
Say she be mute and will not speak a word;
Then I'll commend her volubility,
And say she uttereth piercing eloquence:
If she do bid me pack, I'll give her thanks,
As though she bid me stay by her a week:
If she deny to wed, I'll crave the day
When I shall ask the banns, and when be married.[2]

The divine spark that makes it possible for a salesman

to be a self-starter is enthusiasm. There are many who feel that people are either born with or without this spark, and nothing can be done about it. But, in my opinion, the spark is present in everyone, and if there is any evidence of divinity in human beings it is this particular spark.

The spark may be lying dormant; it may never be fanned into a flame. Circumstances and opportunities vary with individuals. Some may have been exposed to excellent methods of developing it into a real blaze, while others may have had no such experience.

With this spark of enthusiasm properly developed, most of the difficulties of selling are overcome. Without it, selling is a drudgery.

Do not confuse enthusiasm with noise and display of emotion. Enthusiasm may be evidenced by these outward indications, but on the other hand enthusiasm may be a deep-seated passion without any outward display. It isn't what you show; it's what you feel that tells the story of whether or not you have really developed your spark of enthusiasm.

Harry Moock, vice president, Plymouth Motor Corporation, is paid an immense salary because of his enthusiasm and because of his ability to inspire enthusiasm in others. The same is true of all great leaders, regardless of their purpose or their objectives, whether right or wrong; enthusiasm for a principle or a cause has upset governments and changed the map of the world.

John H. Patterson's enthusiasm for the National Cash Register built one of the greatest institutions in the country and established the principle of scientific training of salesmen on a major scale for the first time in history. He not only had enthusiasm; he had the ability to impart it.

Knute Rockne achieved fame as perhaps America's

greatest football coach because of this outstanding quality
and because he had the ability to impart his enthusiasm
to the members of his team. He probably fashioned his pep
talks on the words of King Henry V, who said:

> *Once more unto the breach, dear friends, once more;*
> *Or close the wall up with our English dead.*
> *In peace there's nothing so becomes a man*
> *As modest stillness and humility:*
> *But when the blast of war blows in our ears,*
> *Then . . .*
> *Stiffen the sinews, summon up the blood,*
> *Disguise fair nature with hard-favour'd rage;*
> *Then lend the eye a terrible aspect.*[3]

Whatever his faults, Adolph Hitler reached his present
position of power because of his enthusiasm for a cause
and his remarkable ability to transfer that enthusiasm to
his listeners.

William Jennings Bryan, a practically unknown young
lawyer from Nebraska, in the National Democratic Convention in Chicago in 1896, swept the delegates off their
feet by his address which ended with this sentence: "You
shall not press down upon the brow of labor this crown of
thorns. You shall not crucify mankind upon a cross of
gold." His cause has been variously described as a fight for
free and unlimited coinage of silver, a fight for the labor-
ing man, a fight for equal rights for all; but, regardless of
what the fight was for, his ability to move men as he did
move them was due to his remarkable enthusiasm.

Outstanding business men and salesmen the world over
love their work and get their greatest pleasure out of it
because of the fact that they have developed their enthusiasm to a very high degree of potency.

We all know hundreds of instances of the success of men whose outstanding qualities were their enthusiasm and their ability to arouse men to action.

Shakespeare has truly said:

> *There's a divinity that shapes our ends,*
> *Rough-hew them how we will.*[4]

We need more men in America with imagination and enthusiasm.

One of our great boasted virtues, common sense, has probably done more to interfere with the progress of civilization than any other force. Imagination and enthusiasm caused Alexander Graham Bell to develop the telephone; common sense said it couldn't work. Imagination and enthusiasm kept the Wright brothers busy on their plans to complete a heavier-than-air machine that would fly when all of their associates' strong common sense advised them to give up the project.

Marconi discovered the wireless because he was not deterred by men with common sense who said that his experiments would be useless, because Marconi had both imagination and enthusiasm.

A salesman with great enthusiasm for his product visualizes the many needs for it. His enthusiasm puts his imagination to work. Salesmen with great enthusiasm for their products or the services they sell refuse to see pictures of failure. They visualize the prospect doing the thing they want him to do. Their enthusiasm brooks no obstacles.

Enthusiasm is synonymous with the "will to win." Is there anything on earth that sweeps people off their feet like enthusiasm? The man who says: "I can't be enthusiastic" is either physically or mentally ill. How can a man sell anything continuously without being enthusiastic?

How can a man be a salesman without being enthusiastic about his job? He's got the finest job in the world; he is selling a fine product; and he's working for himself. He gets enthusiastic about his growth, about his development, about his increasing importance, about his ever widening circle of friends, and his increase of income.

Every time he has a new opportunity, he says: "Now I can try out something different and I will grow; I will learn how to do this thing better," and he bubbles over with enthusiasm.

Enthusiasm brings us definite rewards in every phase of our human activity. The salesman who can feel really enthusiastic about meeting a stranger often builds out of that meeting a strong friend and customer. Greeting people with enthusiasm naturally makes them think you feel they are important and worth knowing. This reaction makes them like you.

The acceptance of advice or presents or favors with enthusiasm does the same thing. Enthusiasm brings optimism instead of pessimism. We naturally seek people who are optimistic and enthusiastic. Those of us who may feel depressed and pessimistic at times certainly are not benefited by meeting other depressed and pessimistic people.

Some may have had to fight since childhood to save their tiny spark—protect it from being extinguished. Parents either help this spark to develop, or by bad judgment, try to put it out. Wise parents encourage both imagination and enthusiasm in their children. Foolish parents shush-shush all manifestations of either.

Schoolteachers can be of great help by encouraging

children to develop this spark. They sometimes do the opposite. Wet blankets at home or at school are very detrimental to fire. And this spark of enthusiasm is at least a semi-divine fire in embryo.

Portia in her plea to Shylock to be merciful shows enthusiasm in an intense but quiet way:

> *The quality of mercy is not strain'd,*
> *It droppeth as the gentle rain from heaven*
> *Upon the place beneath: it is twice blest;*
> *It blesseth him that gives, and him that takes:*
> *'Tis mightiest in the mightiest; it becomes*
> *The throned monarch better than his crown;*
> *His sceptre shows the force of temporal power,*
> *The attribute to awe and majesty,*
> *Wherein doth sit the dread and fear of kings;*
> *But mercy is above this sceptred sway;*
> *It is enthroned in the hearts of kings,*
> *It is an attribute to God himself;*
> *And earthly power doth then show likest God's*
> *When mercy seasons justice.*[5]

Shakespeare knew the value of enthusiasm and knowing it proved it by many of his characters.

Why will enthusiasm help us to win? Because it creates intense desire to accomplish definite purposes; because it furnishes the driving force to our brain to seek solutions of our problems.

We will always have problems.

Enthusiasm will help us to open our minds and solve them.

OPEN-MINDEDNESS

HORATIO: *O day and night, but this is wondrous*
strange!

HAMLET: *And therefore as a stranger give it*
welcome.
There are more things in heaven and
earth, Horatio,
Than are dreamt of in your philosophy.[1]

Probably one of the most important characteristics, sometimes possessed only in a small degree by ordinary salesmen, is open-mindedness.

Someone has truly said, "The ability of the average salesman to close his mind to suggestions or ideas that would improve his technique or benefit him—if such suggestions or ideas seem difficult or disagreeable—is truly amazing."

Shakespeare's ability to keep an open mind was one of his greatest qualifications to a special seat in the hall of famous salesmen.

By having an open mind he was able to receive ideas from all the ordinary, accepted channels of information.

By having an unusually wide-open mind, he had a greater receptivity to all sources—sources that are not as yet discernible to ordinary human beings. This quality alone would rate him as a great salesman.

The profits of a salesman are greatly affected by his ability to receive impressions and to transmute them into definite plans of action.

In order to make salesmanship profitable and really worth while, salesmen must develop the power of receptivity and imagination. They must be able to analyze situations and visualize a prospect's needs. They must have developed a sensitivity to all stimuli and be able to sense the prospect's frame of mind—in other words, recognize the so-called "psychological moment."

Some fairly successful salesmen simply rely on the law of averages—see a certain number of prospects, tell them what you have to sell, ask them to buy. So many calls, so many interviews, so many sales, and so much commission.

They do not have and make no effort to develop a prospect sense. Their minds are closed and they are not interested in successful plans used by others, individual success stories, or proven plans of successful selling. Nor do they take to any form of philosophy or teaching that has helped change ordinary salesmen into super-salesmen almost overnight. To understand, use, and apply the law of affirmative thinking would be a waste of time and effort in their opinion. It would be just so much "hooey."

But once in a while a genius develops suddenly—one who does not pretend to be a genius but who has simply used an intelligent plan of operation. When Clay Hamlin of Buffalo, New York, wrote over $20,000,000 life insurance in a single year, he created a sensation. Many and various were the reactions. From the normal production of $250,000 he had skyrocketed to fame. He had learned how to use his time intelligently in the right places because he was open-minded and enterprising.

He had listened to what his boss had suggested. Charles Monser of Johnson and Monser, general agents for the Mutual Benefit Life Insurance Company for western New York, for whom Mr. Hamlin worked, wanted him to raise his sights and go after larger policies. Mr. Monser outlined the plan to me which he had suggested to Mr. Hamlin. Briefly, here it is:

Call upon one man a month who can buy and pay for a $1,000,000 life insurance policy; total exposure, twelve men per year and $12,000,000 insurance.

Call upon two men a month who can buy and pay for a $500,000 policy of life insurance; total exposure, twenty-four men a year and $12,000,000 insurance.

Call upon four men a month who can buy and pay for a $250,000 policy; total exposure, forty-eight men a year and $12,000,000 insurance.

Call upon ten men a month who can buy and pay for a $100,000 policy; total exposure, 120 men a year and $12,000,000 insurance.

Call on twenty men a month who can buy and pay for a $50,000 policy; total exposure 240 men a year and $12,-000,000 insurance.

Call on forty men a month who can buy and pay for a $25,000 policy of life insurance; total exposure, 480 men a year and $12,000,000 insurance.

The grand total exposure was to be 924 men and $72,-000,000 insurance.

The law of averages suggests one prospect out of ten will buy: therefore, exposure to 924 men and $72,000,000 insurance might produce 92.4 men who will buy $7,200,-000 insurance.

According to Mr. Monser, Mr. Hamlin followed this plan and wrote about $5,600,000. Later he again raised his sights and wrote over $20,000,000. Many of his policies were for several millions each. Much of his business had to be placed with other companies, but he kept in the top rank of Mutual Benefit agents.

There were certain other phases to this plan:

(1) Every working day in the year be in the presence of a prospect who can buy life insurance at 9 o'clock in the morning.

(2) Continue appointments every hour.

(3) Have lunch with someone who can tell you about or introduce you to men of means.

(4) Use at least three evenings a week calling upon prospects.

I might mention that the adoption of this plan by Mr. Hamlin brought great financial rewards to him; but it did more than that. His company, the Mutual Benefit Life Insurance Company of Newark, New Jersey, saw in him a great leader and developer of manpower and appointed him general agent to succeed Johnson and Monser in western New York.

Don MacKinnon, special Detroit representative of the Provident Mutual Life Insurance Company, testified before a large group of life underwriters there that a modification of the plan worked for him, and he quadrupled his business in a single year.

He selected prospects from many of the classes mentioned by Mr. Monser. He made a list of them and classified them, putting this list under the plate glass top of his table. He called them members of his "Life Insurance Club," and, as Mr. MacKinnon says, he called on them "to collect their dues to the club." A systematic plan or supervision of his own soliciting in a more profitable field brought worth-while results.

Both Mr. MacKinnon and Mr. Hamlin were following a sure-fire rule in selling:

Identify your market, select good prospects, arrange them in order of their importance to you, then expose yourself to them so they will have a chance to buy from you. Make these exposures frequently.

This technique never fails.

I have on various occasions praised Mr. Hamlin and recommended his plan. Thousands have heard me. Only a few have adopted the plan in good faith and carried it out. Those who did have materially increased their income.

But what of the others—literally thousands? They continue to plod along the same beaten track. Their minds are closed to new ideas, new plans, better methods.

"What was good enough for my father was good enough for me" has prevented millions from developing better plans or adopting new ideas.

Salesmen have only two things to sell—their time and their ability. Since the amount of time in each day is fixed, nothing can be done to increase it, but much can be done to make its use more effective. Expending the same amount of time on better prospects will pay big dividends.

Planned interviews and reducing the time of each call will create a surplus of time, which can be used elsewhere with profit. Your ability is strictly your own problem. It is whatever you want it to be. Increased efficiency and sales technique will pay big dividends. However, even with these you can't reach the top rung of efficiency without development of your receptivity to ideas. And to receive ideas you must keep your avenues of thought ever open.

"Practice makes perfect" is a good adage, especially when applied to opening your mind to helpful suggestions. Begin today by asking yourself these questions: What is it that more successful salesmen have that I do not have? What is wrong with me? How can I help myself to improve?

Read the collected works of William Shakespeare and profit by a statement such as this:

> *There is a tide in the affairs of men*
> *Which taken at the flood leads on to fortune.*[2]

But to know when the "tide" is at the "flood" presupposes knowledge and a sensitivity to relative things.

Shakespeare had the ability to catch from casual contacts and conversations of ordinary types of human beings something far greater than what they said or did. His imagination worked with a will. His mind went on when others stopped talking. He sensed the flood tide and made his fortune.

Did you ever pass and repass a famous building and never notice how many steps there were? You did not observe the building carefully. Do you know why? Because you were not interested. If you are interested you will observe and concentrate, and you will know.

Shakespeare's power of observation and concentration appeared to be supernatural. But these powers were developed because of his intense interest in all things in life. He had an open mind and great receptivity to all ideas from the ordinary and accepted channels of information.

He also apparently had an open channel to sources of information that to many would seem supernatural. He was so prolific in his ideas that many people find it hard to believe one man could accomplish so much in so short a time.

He understood the full meaning of the opening line of Hamlet's soliloquy: *To be, or not to be.*[3]

Whether "to be," which translated into everyday language means to live in the full sense of the word, or "not to be" is a question each individual must answer for himself or herself.

With an open mind and great receptivity to progressive ideas life will present to us rich rewards. With a closed mind we only exist.

HUMAN UNDERSTANDING

The quality of mercy is not strain'd.[1]

Pope has truly said: "The proper study of mankind is man."[2]

And no man ever made a more thorough study of man than William Shakespeare. In the higher walks of life, among the middle classes, and in society's dregs, he studied men. He studied their strength and their weaknesses, their emotions and reactions, the motives that would move them to action—

Whether placid, or on edge;

Whether stolid or responsive;

Calm and strong or excitable and weak;

Tender or brutal;

Forgiving or relentless;

Kind or cruel;

Generous or greedy;

Stable or ambitious.

Certain motives would make them take action, and his plays produce characters that not only possess these characteristics but express them in words.

So Shakespeare understanding all types of human

beings speaks to us through these puppets so that we, too, may understand all reactions of men and profit thereby.

What a clinic for an ambitious salesman!

What a laboratory for men and women who want to know life and mankind!

> *Or that the Everlasting had not fix'd*
> *His canon 'gainst self-slaughter!*[3]

When Hamlet in his soliloquy cries out against the divine ban placed upon self-destruction, he voices an emotion old as life itself. When melancholy sweeps down upon us, we are apt to begin to think of an easy way out. But Shakespeare points out in another speech of Hamlet well considered reasons against self-slaughter.

> *To die, to sleep;*
> *To sleep: perchance to dream: ay, there's the rub;*
> *For in that sleep of death, what dreams may come,*
> *When we have shuffled off this mortal coil,*
> *Must give us pause.*[4]

And again:

> *The undiscover'd country from whose bourn*
> *No traveller returns, puzzles the will,*
> *And makes us rather bear those ills we have*
> *Than fly to others that we know not of.*[5]

With his deep understanding of human ills, he knew that melancholy leads to insanity, and it is no wonder that Shakespeare cried out against the failure of the medical profession to find a cure for incipient insanity:

MACBETH: *Canst thou not minister to a mind diseased,*
Pluck from the memory a rooted sorrow?

DOCTOR: *Therein the patient*
Must minister to himself.

MACBETH: *Throw physic to the dogs, I'll none of it.*[6]

This great problem is put in our laps, where it belongs, with the statement: "Therein the patient must minister to himself."

In order to minister to ourselves properly, we must control our mental attitude. If only more salesmen could understand that this self-slaughter, of which Hamlet speaks, also applies to their persistent efforts to "slaughter" themselves, their time, their efficiency, and occasionally their prospects!

This self-slaughter takes place when the salesman refuses to prepare, makes a poor approach, a bad presentation, and ends without tact or judgment. Verily, salesmen should pray that the "Everlasting" fix "his canon 'gainst" their slaughter of themselves.

Why should we look on the dark side of life? Why show failure pictures on our mental screen? Why become downhearted and pessimistic? After all, as Shakespeare says:

> *There is nothing either good or bad,*
> *but thinking makes it so.*[7]

We do not feel any better by talking and complaining about the weather. There has been a lot said about it but as no one has ever been able to do anything about it, why discuss it?

Our job is to tackle problems that, no matter how tough, offer a better chance of solution. And to solve them we must first believe they can be solved. Our mental attitude must be right. We must minister to ourselves.

Shakespeare also understood the driving power of vanity. King Lear demands of his three daughters expressions of love and admiration. Goneril and Regan comply with expressions such as these:

> GONERIL: *Sir, I love you more than words can wield the matter,*
> *Dearer than eye-sight, space and liberty.*[8]

Then REGAN says:

> *I am made of that self metal as my sister,*
> *And prize me at her worth.*[9]

While CORDELIA, being honest, says:

> *Good my lord,*
> *You have begot me, bred me, loved me: I*
> *Return those duties back as are right fit,*
> *Obey you, love you, and most honour you.*
> *Why have my sisters husbands, if they say*
> *They love you all? Haply, when I shall wed,*
> *That lord whose hand must take my plight shall carry*
> *Half my love with him, half my care and duty:*
> *Sure, I shall never marry like my sisters,*
> *To love my father all.*[10]

Goneril and Regan received vast estates from King Lear. Cordelia received only truth for her dower. But, remember this, King Lear came to grief because, as Shakespeare says:

> *He that loves to be flattered*
> *is worthy o' the flatterer.*[11]

Shakespeare was a realist. He knew men. And he knew that if you want to get along with them on the best possible basis you must not deflate their egos, but commend them and so appeal to their vanity.

Now a number of supposedly bright salesmen say this: "You are all wet," or "You are dead wrong about that and I'll prove it to you."

Just remember this: a man's opinion is the child of his brain and he values it highly—sometimes more highly than his own flesh and blood. Don't tell him his "brain child" is an idiot. And don't PROVE it. Quote Shakespeare, thus:

Good reasons must of force give place to better,[12]

and while admitting his reasons or opinions are good, suggest that they are based on his knowledge of the facts and that you would like to present additional facts.

The best definition I know of selling is "making people want to do what you want them to do," because most of us, as far as is possible, do the thing we want to do in about the way we want to do it. Making people want to do a thing means that we must associate the doing of that thing with success, happiness, growth, profit, and pleasure. And it is easier to do this by working with a prospect, according to his own nature, than to fight his natural inclinations. Trying to force him against his own nature is not only uphill work but very unprofitable.

You would not try to sell a man a racing car when he loathes racing and high speeds. You would not ask a fat man to walk two miles to look at a piece of property you wanted to sell him!

You will note in Shakespeare's plays how well he handled the relationship of a vast assortment of human beings.

Along the line of adaptability and human understanding, one of the things that Shakespeare knew so well how to handle in his plays was the relationship between different sorts of human beings. He appreciated it as very few people do and understood the futility of trying to make people do things against their own natures. In other words, he did not advocate talking rapidly to a slow thinker because he knew that a slow thinker does not get ideas quickly, loses the thread of the matter, and consequently is immune to suggestion. If a salesman deals with a slow thinker he must be sure he suits the tempo of his conversation to the tempo of the thinking of the listener. Many a salesman loses the interest of his buyer merely because he does not speak the language of the buyer.

For example, a salesman is talking to a farmer who has had very little experience in handling sums of cash. Money to him is a symbol and not an actual thing with which he is familiar. However, he is familiar with the things he raises, such as grain and livestock. The smart salesman translates his statements into the language of the buyer. As an illustration, in talking to a farmer about the cost of insurance or an automobile or a refrigerator, instead of speaking of $50 or $100, say to him in his language: "If you would like to have this new refrigerator, all it would cost you would be about three hogs the size of the 400-pound one over there. Now, Mr. Jones, you would surely be willing to raise three extra hogs in order to get this electric refrigerator which would be a great saving to your wife because much of the food now being wasted could be preserved by the use of this refrigerator."

Years ago my daughter came into the house laughing very vigorously and when asked what she was laughing about said: "Fanny was here with a lot of little kids and said to me, 'Would you please show these here little children them there little fish?' "

I asked her what was wrong with that. Her reply was: "But that is such bad English."

I explained that Fanny was German and had asked her in English to do her a favor, and I suggested to my daughter that she run out and tell Fanny in German that she would be very glad to show the children the fish. "But," she said, "I don't speak German."

My reply was: "I don't either, so Fanny seems to be smarter than either one of us. She can speak both German and English, but we cannot answer her in her own language." Similarly, many salesmen fail to learn the simple lesson of speaking the language of the buyer.

Suppose, for example, you were talking to a person who has no mechanical sense, and you happen to be trying to sell him an automobile. You might just as well speak a foreign language as to talk about the construction of the engine, the revolutions per minute, or the stroke of the piston. Mechanical terms mean nothing to him, and if you get into a mechanical discussion he probably will tune you out permanently so that you will fail to make the sale. On the other hand, if you discuss with him the fact this particular automobile will get him to the place he wants to go with the least possible effort and the least possible cost, that he will come home from a trip less tired because the car handles so simply and easily, that due to the very exceptional construction, this is a car which will practically never wear out, you are talking the language of that particular buyer.

If you are trying to get on a basis of friendly relationship or adapt yourself to some of his peculiarities, tell him a story like this:

"A young couple got married and successfully eluded the bridal party by escaping unnoticed to their Pullman car, side-tracked at a station, and into their stateroom unobserved except by the porter. Calling the porter into the stateroom, they asked him to clean up the rice and then the bridegroom said to the porter, 'Here is $5.00 and I want you to do us a favor. Nobody knows that we are on the train and nobody knows that we are newly married except you. Now, we are not going to act like a newly married couple so we won't be annoyed by unpleasant attention, but you will have to keep our secret. If you do not let anybody know we are married, when we get to our destination I will give you an extra $5.00. Do you understand?"

"Yes, boss, Ah sure does an you can count on me. Ah'll keep it dark, won't tell a soul."

But the next morning, on their return from the dining car to their stateroom, practically all of the passengers were looking at them from behind their magazines and newspapers with slightly quizzical and critical looks. This, of course, annoyed the bridegroom so he rang for the porter and said,

"You are a fine porter. I gave you $5.00 to keep secret the fact we are newly married and apparently you have gone up and down every aisle announcing it. We are being annoyed to death."

"No sah, boss, no sah, that is just what Ah didn't do. Some of these ladies back here in your car did ask me if you were newlyweds, and Ah told them, no indeedy, you wasn't married at all. You was just chums, that's all—just chums."

Many years ago when I was general agent of the Provident Mutual Life Insurance Company, I acquired one of the dumbest agents I ever knew. He knew less about more things than any human being I had ever met except a girl. This girl not only didn't know anything, she didn't even suspect anything.

I discovered in the course of handling men that sales managers sometimes make the error of thinking the proper way to develop morale and enthusiasm is to give their salesmen a pep talk every morning or once a week. I decided, however, after several years, that a great many of our salesmen tuned us out and didn't hear what we said, so we had no way of finding out whether they were putting into operation the sales suggestions we had made.

Therefore, I decided to change all this by holding a morning meeting in which I gave all the salesmen a chance to tell me how they had handled their prospects the day before—in other words, what they said and what they did when in the field.

One day at such a meeting after the salesmen had recounted their experiences, I told them one of mine. I related how I went out to Grant Street to see a man named Thompson. He was thirty-two years old, had a wife and three-year-old child. I presented to him the facts about a life insurance policy, called a twenty-payment endowment at age sixty-five. I explained to him that he paid a premium for twenty years, received a dividend each year, and that, if living at sixty-five, the company would pay him $5,000 or, if he died before age sixty-five, the company would pay his widow $5,000 and all this protection was offered for a yearly premium of $160.60. However, the more I talked the less interested he became and finally I had to give up without getting an application. Then I asked the salesmen if they knew what I had done wrong.

No one knew but the dumb salesman. He was a man

who never wrote any business, but could tell the other fellow how to do it. I said to him: "I suppose had you been there you could have secured this application." His reply was: "Yes, I think I would have."

So I said sarcastically: "Here is the application with everything on it except the signature. All you have to do is see Mr. Thompson, get his signature, get him examined, get the check, and it is your business with full commission, payable to you."

The embarrassing thing about this story is he did get it, and I had to give him a chance to tell the other salesmen how he did it. He said: "I went out to see Mr. Thompson and asked him if Mr. Burruss had called on him the day before and his answer was 'yes.' I asked Mr. Thompson if Mr. Burruss had explained to him that when he reached age sixty-five he would get a check for $5,000. His answer was 'yes.' I asked him if he was sure he understood it. 'If I am living at age sixty-five I will get a check for $5,000,' Mr. Thompson said.

" 'Now, did Mr. Burruss explain to you that if you died before you reached age sixty-five your widow would get a check for $5,000? Do you understand it? Let's see.'

" 'Yes,' he said. 'If I die before I reach the age of sixty-five, my widow gets a check for $5,000.'

"I said, 'That is fine. You do understand it.'

" 'Now, did Mr. Burruss tell you that you give me your check for $160.60?'

" 'Yes,' he said.

" 'Well, now what do you do?'

" 'I give you my check for $160.60,' and he did."

I then asked my salesman what was wrong with my presentation. He answered, "I asked Mr. Thompson that and he replied, 'Well, Mr. Burruss talked so fast I never had a chance to catch up with him.' "

So indeed Shakespeare understood the slow-thinking salesman and the fast-thinking one, as well as understanding the salesman who is a conscientious objector—the type that lets his thinking stop his doing, or as Hamlet says:

> *Thus conscience doth make cowards of us all,*
> *And thus the native hue of resolution*
> *Is sicklied o'er with the pale cast of thought,*
> *And enterprises of great pitch and moment*
> *With this regard their currents turn awry*
> *And lose the name of action.*[13]

Letting thoughts stop us when we are on our way to success is foolish. They may be excellent thoughts or they may be the kind of thoughts Shakespeare had in mind when he said:

> *A thought which, quarter'd, hath but one part wisdom*
> *And ever three parts coward.*[14]

One of the many things that interfere with salesmen's progress, and in some instances cause discouragement and defeat, is getting in debt. Salesmen accept advances without realizing they are piling up a debt that must sooner or later be paid. And unpleasantness usually follows.

Again a word to the wise from the wisest. Shakespeare has Polonius say to his son, when that son was starting out on his career:

> *Neither a borrower nor a lender be:*
> *For a loan oft loses both itself and friend.*[15]

AN ALL-OUT EFFORT FOR SUCCESS

The fault, dear Brutus, is not in our stars,
But in ourselves, that we are underlings.[1]

The world offers us any degree of success, but she asks payment in full. Some salesmen do not want to pay the full price and so do not achieve full success. Shakespeare points out to us some of the extra qualities we should cultivate, for example:

PERSISTENCE

When Shakespeare has the Duke of Gloucester stop the funeral procession of King Henry VI and woo Lady Anne, the chief mourner, after her many repeated rebuffs,[2] he gives a striking example of persistence in the face of overwhelming odds.

Lady Anne knows the Duke is a murderer. She knows he killed her husband and the king.

The Duke is unsightly, misshapened, and ugly. But with all the odds against him, by persistence alone he finally wins her.

This, of course, was an unworthy cause, but even in an unworthy cause persistence gets results. While I do not recommend it in an unworthy cause, I do recommend persistence in a worthy cause, and salesmen to succeed must persist.

When Cassius wins Brutus to the conspiracy,[3] he, too, employs skilled salesmanship and persistence.

When Othello, the Moor, wins Desdemona and the approval of the rulers of Venice,[4] he, too, gives a truly remarkable example of persistence and salesmanship.

Another striking illustration of persistence is the fact that it was Lady Macbeth who forced Macbeth to do all the murderous things he did. Speaking of her husband, she says:

> *That I may pour my spirits in thine ear*
> *And chastise with the valour of my tongue*
> *All that impedes thee.*[5]

She thus changed the nature of Macbeth from being too *full o' the milk of human kindness*[6] to a murderous monster.

Yes, persistence is like the continuous drop of water that wears away the stone, the power of erosion that has made canyons out of mountainous country. It can and will make geniuses out of dullards—and a salesman out of you, no matter what you think.

ADAPTABILITY

The unerring ability of a cat to land on its feet is not nearly so remarkable as the ability of a salesman to adapt himself quickly to a situation or a set of circumstances suddenly thrust upon him. This requires more than agility of body. It requires mental agility, mental resources, vast abundance of information, thorough understanding of human nature, sense of humor, sound philosophy of life.

There is only one place where a salesman can learn all this—only one textbook that completely covers all of it. And that is a book entitled, *The Complete Works of William Shakespeare.*

FORCE

There is a time for wit, there is a time for tact, persuasion, and appeal. But to really make a success of your life, to gain wealth, power, and prestige, you must have force—force of character.

The pages of Shakespeare are replete with forceful characters, those who could by force dominate scenes and situations. Whether we think of Petruchio dominating and taming the fiery Katharina, or the dignified force of Brutus controlling Cassius in his outbursts, or King Henry V urging his men to battle, we find Shakespeare always capable of proving to us the value of force.

We must be forceful if we are to be convincing. Persuasion is essential, but without force there is no conviction, and where there are no force and conviction, there are no sales.

USE OF SUGGESTION

IAGO: *Ha! I like not that.*

OTHELLO: *What dost thou say?*

IAGO: *Nothing, my lord: or if—I know not what.*[7]

Shakespeare was a master of subtle suggestion because he understood that once a suggestion has been made, once it is on its way, it should not be interfered with—or any other suggestions made. Shakespeare, in the words of Iago, shows the master touch, planting suggestions to corrupt the thinking of the fair and open-minded Othello.

Cassius talking to Brutus cleverly plants the suggestion that Caesar may be crowned king and despotism may again flourish in Rome.

The King drops suggestions in the mind of Laertes that cause him to kill Hamlet.

The witches pour suggestions of his future greatness in the ear of Macbeth. He is changed by them and seeks to make the suggestions come true.

The law of suggestion as an aid to selling is as powerful as the law of gravitation, and no one used it with greater skill than Shakespeare.

MAKING THE VOICE WORK FOR YOU

*Speak the speech, . . . as **I** pronounced it to you, trippingly on the tongue.*[1]

Shakespeare knew salesmanship!

He knew salesmen.

He knew: How careless they were in dress and appearance; how they made bad approaches and sloppy sales presentations; how they sometimes failed to use the power of suggestion, or set up a standard of measurement and commit a prospect to it; how they at times overlooked an appeal to the buying motives of a prospect or failed to get action and a settlement.

But his understanding of the necessary qualifications of a top notch salesman went deeper than that. He knew what the average sales manager does not know, or knowing, does not put into practice. He knew that the human voice can be made a great asset or a tremendous liability. He knew that the quality of the speaking voice can make selling easy. It can also make selling difficult or even impossible.

How many voices have you heard that irritate you?

To how many people have you listened without understanding them, due to poor enunciation and improper articulation?

How many salesmen can you recall whose voices failed to ring true? How many failed to convince you because their voices lacked force, sincerity, and conviction? Careless, irritating, unconvincing, unpleasant, and disagreeable voices that could have worked for them instead of against them defeat many salesmen.

Due to the failure to recognize the value of the proper kind of speaking voice and its proper use, salesmen fail.

Men excel animals in two things: they think and talk.

Salesmen should excel other men by thinking better and faster. They should also use their voices to talk more pleasingly and more effectively. It is a vital part of a salesman's equipment.

Shakespeare tells how to use the voice so as to get results, when he has Hamlet say to the players:

> *Speak the speech, I pray you, as I pronounced it to you, trippingly on the tongue: but if you mouth it, as many of your players do, I had as lief the town-crier spoke my lines.*[2]

Clear, decisive speech is paramount—with no careless, sloppy mouthing of words.

If salesmen would only realize how easily they could increase their income, improve their business and social relations, and win for themselves more friends, by using their speaking voices as Shakespeare recommends, we would have a lot of witnesses who could testify to the effectiveness of Shakespeare's sales suggestions.

*Nor do not saw the air too much with your hand,
thus; but use all gently: for in the very torrent,
tempest, and, as I may say, whirlwind of your passion, you must acquire and beget a temperance that
may give it smoothness.*[3]

Here again salesmen are properly advised in their manner of presentation. To overdo is to undo, and many a
poor salesman has lost his job because he failed to use
the finesse so aptly suggested. He was too vigorous—
too demonstrative. He jumped at his prospects—too much
sounding brass and not enough seductive, soft music, that
would help to get acceptance.

Successful golf players succeed because of proper coor-
dination of mind, eye, arms, hands, legs, feet, and body.

Why isn't salesmanship as important as golf?

Why not, as Shakespeare suggests, use all our faculties
to do a real job of selling?

*Suit the action to the word,
the word to the action . . .*[4]

In order to do this as nearly perfectly as possible, it is
well to know first what you are going to say.

Too many salesmen and too many speakers are troubled
at times because they do not know what to say. Their
preparation was faulty, and so their performance is bad.
Many salesmen trust to God to tell them what to say, and
God being so busy coming to the aid of so many helpless
and incompetent salesmen does not always tell them in
time!

The salesman who has a planned sales presentation can
spend a lot of time profitably practicing delivery of that
presentation and so achieve better results.

The same thing applies to many so-called speakers. Hurried and careless preparation of the speech to be made—or reading the speech in a dull, uninteresting way —causes the listening audience to react unfavorably.

A critic who was asked by such a careless speaker for his reaction to the speech said:

"There were three things wrong with your speech: first, you read it; second, you read it badly; third, it was not worth reading in the first place."

Some salesmen fail to "suit the action to the word and the word to the action."

They sometimes forget that selling means getting favorable action and, consequently, favorable acceptance.

There are two types of salesmen—the fox terrier type and the cat type.

The fox terrier type is too effervescent. He is impatient. He cannot wait. Like a fox terrier he leaps at you.

Consider this possible situation:

Put a mouse and a fox terrier in a room together, with a hole in the baseboard deep enough to protect the mouse from the dog, but no way for either of them to escape.

The fox terrier will never catch the mouse.

Why? Because he cannot wait for the mouse to come out.

The minute the mouse starts out of his hole, the fox terrier jumps at him, barking wildly. The mouse runs back in the hole.

And so it is with this type of salesman. He, too, cannot wait. When a customer says to him: "I don't like your house," the fox terrier salesman barks loudly:

"Is that so! Well, you are all wet and I'll prove it!"

He thus drives the customer back into his hole.

Or the customer makes some other criticism. Again the

salesman leaps at him and again the customer retreats. The salesman has forgotten—if he ever knew—the advice of the old master, Bill Shakespeare:

> *Give every man thy ear, but few thy voice:*
> *Take each man's censure, but reserve thy judgement.*[5]

If he has followed the above advice he has become more like a cat in his selling. He stops, looks, and listens. He makes no unnecessary movements. He talks less and listens more. He waits for an opening. He waits for the psychological moment.

Let us consider the situation if we substitute a cat for the fox terrier in the room with the mouse.

The cat will always catch the mouse.

Why? Because the cat is patient and cautious. It makes no false moves. The mouse comes out of the hole and runs back. The cat lies still. The mouse comes out and turns a flip-flop. Still the cat makes no move. But let the mouse come out just six inches too far, and it is goodbye little mouse.

So acts the cat salesman—the one who profits by Bill Shakespeare.

The customer says: "I don't like your house."

The cat salesman says: "I am sorry, but I am sure if I were in your place and received the same treatment, I would not like it either. Now tell me frankly, what have we done to you?"

The customer will, mouse-like, come out into the open, and the salesman has a chance to get the facts. And having the facts he is in a position to satisfy the customer and change a potential enemy into a friend.

Salesmen who want to win use the technique of the cat

and find out just what is going on in the prospect's mind.

If you happen to know anyone who plays poker, ask him this question: "Do you, when playing poker, ever try to scare a player when he starts out on a limb?"

The answer, I am sure, will be in the negative. He will say: "No, I always let him get out on the end of the limb, before I saw it off."

There is a type of so-called salesman for whom Shakespeare wrote these words:

> *And let those that play your clowns*
> *speak no more than is set down for them.*[6]

These foolish or clown salesmen use speech to conceal not to reveal thought. Overzealous as they are in the abundant use of words, they should have their speech or sales talk "set down for them."

In other words, they should stick to their planned sales presentation. Otherwise, they begin from nowhere and end there. They are truly "Gratianos," and Shakespeare had them in mind when he said:

> *Gratiano speaks an infinite deal of nothing, more*
> *than any man in all Venice. His reasons are as two*
> *grains of wheat hid in two bushels of chaff: you*
> *shall seek all day ere you find them: and when you*
> *have them, they are not worth the search.*[7]

These so-called salesmen are not an asset to an organization or firm. They make few sales, although they take up as much space and more time than first-class salesmen.

They are distinct liabilities. They spoil many sales. They lose friends for the house. They make it tough for all other salesmen. They annoy, bore, and antagonize prospects by the thousands. They create resistance for those that follow no matter what their line. They are responsible for the many curt reports of secretaries, when other salesmen call.

"Mr. Jones is busy."

"Mr. Jones is Out," with a capital "O."

"Mr. Jones is not interested."

In other words, Mr. Jones cannot afford to take a chance. After all he, too, must make a living. His time is limited and organized and so why risk listening to a "windy salesman"? No wonder he sends out an S O S.

Even good salesmen at times make the fatal error of overtalking. They talk a prospect into buying and then continue and talk him out of it. When a sale is made, it's time for the salesman to leave. There is no profit in remaining. But there is a chance for loss, and further conversation may kill the sale.

I remember once after I had closed a sale I made this remark: "If it does not suit you to pay cash, I'll take your note for ninety days."

The prospect replied: "That reminds me! I have a note due at the bank. I can't take it at all."

GOOD ETHICS AND CODE OF PROCEDURE

> *But he that filches from me my good name*
> *Robs me of that which not enriches him*
> *And makes me poor indeed.*[1]

"Anything that I do that gets the business is ethical," says a hard-boiled modern salesman. "And anything my

competitor does that takes it away from me is unethical."
So say those who do not know, or knowing, misinterpret.

A boy, who had an essay to write on ethics, came to his
father with this question: "Dad, what are ethics?"

"I'm glad you came to me, son, with this question," replied his father. "I have made a study of ethics, and today
I have been facing a rather difficult ethical problem. A
man owed us $100. Today he came in and paid me $110
by mistake. Now here is the kernel of this ethical problem.
Shall I keep the overpayment of $10 for myself, or shall
I split it with my partner?"

But Shakespeare points out how a code of procedure
can be made extremely valuable when, through Polonius
to Laertes, he tells us:

> *Costly thy habit as thy purse can buy,*
> *. . . rich, not gaudy:*
> *For the apparel oft proclaims the man.*[2]

If we want people to think we are successful, we must
dress the part. Then many will never know that we are not.

> *Assume a virtue, if you have it not.*[3]

You would not put on your old clothes to go to a bank
to borrow money.

The store that is dressed up gets the business.

The one that is ill-kept is passed by.

The city without smoke is cleaner, better appearing than
the one which has not acted against the smoke nuisance.

Let your apparel proclaim you successful. The road to
success will be made easier.

What has Shakespeare to say about loyalty? Again listen to old Polonius.

> *Those friends thou hast, and their adoption tried,*
> *Grapple them to thy soul with hoops of steel.*[4]

How does this affect you?

Employees who accept a job should not do so unless willing to render every possible service to make their employer's business successful. It is better for you. Unless the business of your employer succeeds, there will not be a job for you. You will feel much better in every way, when you give your best.

Kiss the hand that feeds you, don't bite it.

How about employers? They, too, should recognize this fact. A good rule works both ways.

No man has a right to hire anyone unless he is willing to do his utmost to see that the one he hires succeeds.

National Cash Register Company has a slogan, "He who approaches temptation to a man does him an injury, and if he fails, shares his guilt."

Grapple your employees to you "with hoops of steel." And remember this: you cannot expect loyalty from anyone against his own best interests. So be loyal to him— pay him fairly.

And how about your customers, the buyers? Neither salesmen nor employers could exist without them.

In the final analysis they pay all your overhead—salaries, commissions and profits.

Why not give your customers a break? Tie them to you with hoops of friendship based upon fair and courteous treatment. Help them to reap a profit from their business relations with you.

Polonius continues:

> *Give every man thy ear, . . .*
> *. . . but reserve thy judgement.*[5]

Listen more, talk less, and you will find out what is going on in your prospect's mind. And then Shakespeare has Polonius say to Laertes:

> *This above all: to thine own self be true,*
> *And . . .*
> *Thou canst not then be false to any man.*[6]

What does Shakespeare mean by this? An appeal to loyalty? I think it is more than that. Shakespeare has already had Polonius discuss loyalty. Now he is asking us to be true to ourselves—in other words, be true to the latent talent within us.

Every man has a tremendous amount of ability, untold resources he knows nothing about until accident or chance or something else uncovers them, and he finds he has been untrue to himself because he has never used them. We have tremendous resources that we are not using. We are like a 100-acre field with only 10 acres in cultivation, the other 90 acres going to weeds.

In order to be true to ourselves, we must develop this latent talent within us. We have received this talent in trust, and it is our duty to develop it. If we are true to ourselves, if we do develop it, we cannot then be false to any man.

It doesn't make any difference what your enemies think of you, or what your friends think of you; it is what you know yourself to be that really counts. If you know you are a fourflusher, are not giving your best, and are not delivering the goods, you are not being true to yourself. And you don't get much satisfaction out of that.

I wish I had the power to get over to every man, woman, and child in America that they, too, have a call to be true to themselves in a very special way.

There never has been a time in our history when it was so important.

It has been said that things which cost us little have little value in our minds.

If we are ignorant of values, precious stones are the same as ordinary pebbles. We don't know the difference. Ignorance is a great leveler of values.

Now, value is the amount of want-satisfying power a thing has. If we don't know what it is, it probably has no want-satisfying power. It has no value. We don't know how to use it.

So we should know the American way of living.

We should know how we receive these privileges.

We should also know their value.

Because we have never had occasion to go without these privileges so freely ours in this country, we are not conscious of the fact that we have them.

We are very apt to take their possession for granted.

We never really appreciate the value of the things we have until we lose them.

If America, like some of the countries in Europe, were to lose these privileges for even a short period of time, we would then understand how very valuable they really were. Our freedom, our way of life, means so little to so many of us because:

It apparently costs us nothing.

We have always had it.

We don't know how we got it.

We have no fear of losing it.

So why worry or get excited?

Why do anything to help preserve it?

If we want to be true to ourselves, we will decide now to use some of that latent power to discover what our freedom, our way of life, really is, also the price we had to pay for what we have.

We might examine the records and see what sacrifices our ancestors made—how they obtained freedom bit by bit; how they fought and died to preserve every bit of progress they had made toward the goal of perfect freedom; how they bequeathed that progress to us to guard; how they have urged us to carry on the struggle.

Then carry that message to everyone until it can be truly said that all Americans now know what freedom means—that all Americans appreciate its value—that all Americans are willing to fight for it and, if need be, to die for it.

Then and only then will we truly be "true" to ourselves.

We must be true to ourselves in order not to be false to our country or to anyone else.

SALES TECHNIQUE

All the world's a stage,
And all the men and women merely players:
They have their exits and their entrances;
And one man in his time plays many parts.[1]

We are sometimes apt to think that we have been original and created some new ideas or some new technique in salesmanship. We announce the ideas with a great flare of trumpets. If these sales ideas are good, we are willing to admit that the originator of them must have been a good salesman.

But the man who thought he had originated them may be fooling himself.

My father, defending a college chum of mine for plagiarism, wisely said: "An original thought and a revived memory are so closely kin that it is difficult for anyone to tell them apart."

Yes, many times we think we have originated something only to find it is already in use. Many of the so-called creators of new sales ideas or technique will find their ideas are in reality not original, but merely revived memories.

William Shakespeare gave them to us centuries ago, and he was a good salesman.

For example, the follow-up letter and personal interview system. Let us turn to the pages of Shakespeare and see what he has to offer along this line. If we read our "Julius Caesar" carefully, we will discover that the conspirators used this technique in selling Brutus the idea of joining the conspiracy. You will recall the sales talks given to Brutus by Cassius, and then you will discover that these talks were followed by notes thrown over Brutus' garden wall. These notes were follow-up letters. They read something like this:

"Arise, Brutus, your country needs you." Signed: Pro Bono Publico.

"Caesar is a tyrant, Brutus. Destroy Caesar and set Rome free."

Similar missives were signed anonymously.

The idea of these letters was to make Brutus feel that the whole country was aroused. As a matter of fact, they were merely "propaganda" follow-up letters thrown in his yard by the conspirators themselves.

We have had numerous imitations of this type of follow-up letter propaganda in our country within recent years. A bill is introduced in Congress and certain interests oppose it. But they need wide-spread public disapproval to defeat it.

Suddenly the legislators are swamped with letters opposing it.

A Shakespearean sales idea in modern clothes.

But it gives us a definite and concrete idea of how Shakespeare sold the effectiveness of the personal interview and the follow-up letter system.

So Shakespeare was the salesman.

Let us take another so-called sales discovery—setting up a standard of measurement and committing one to it.

Let us look again at "Julius Caesar," and we find Brutus using this idea in his address to the Romans.

Is it the magic formula of the four laws of a sale created by someone and marketed as an easy lesson in the principles of salesmanship by somebody in Podunk, New Jersey? These laws were well known to Shakespeare and were used by him repeatedly. They were used by Brutus in his speech to the Romans. They were used by Mark Antony who followed Brutus. They are:

(1) Get attention;
(2) Arouse interest;
(3) Create a desire;
(4) Get action.

You shall see later how closely Mark Antony followed these laws in making his great sale to the Roman people.

Is it a book on *Buying Motives and How to Use Them,* that has been suddenly introduced as something new in salesmanship? No salesman who ever lived was a greater master in using buying motives to make people do the thing he wanted them to do than William Shakespeare. He was a master.

Let us note a few of the buying motives and later you will see how Shakespeare has Mark Antony use them effectively—profit, pride, affection, caution, or fear, curiosity, yielding to weakness. The reason I am calling your attention to these buying motives and the qualities of a salesman and to his technique is because I want you to see clearly that all of these qualities and all of this technique were possessed and used by William Shakespeare throughout his works.

Let me give you the application of some of the principles of salesmanship by using the puppets of Shakespeare's creative mind to speak to us in the language of a salesman.

Salesmanship is something more than the mere marketing of merchandise. It is the marketing of ideas.

And sometimes even today in this busy cynical world, it is the marketing of an ideal.

Shakespeare presents selling from all three angles. He gave us a very definite, a very concrete, a very scientific illustration of salesmanship.

Let's take a look.

Pick up your copy of Shakespeare. Turn to the play, "Julius Caesar." The conspirators had gathered. They wanted to get rid of Caesar. They thought of him as a dangerous competitor. They thought that once they were rid of Caesar, their lot or their business would be better. They forgot the old maxim—"your only real competitor is public opinion."

They felt then as a few of us insurance agents felt centuries later when a new life insurance agent came to our town and made a striking success.

"He must be a crook," we said. Why did we say that? Because, otherwise we were incompetent. And that wasn't possible. We justified our own failure. Our alibi closed the door to the solution of the problem.

Caesar was a great success. The conspirators were failures. Therefore, Caesar must be a crook—"too ambitious, too dangerous." And so, Caesar must be disposed of promptly. They could not take away his franchise or license. He did not have one. But they could take away his life. Why not assassinate him? That would be final. No change of administration could help him. "Yes, that's a good idea, assassinate Caesar and we'll take his place," said the conspirators.

Stop a moment and consider.

The conspirators were not popular. Failures rarely are. Their reputations were a handicap, so they decided they must have a leader. He must be a successful man. He must be popular. He must have the confidence and respect of the populace. They must have him. Was there such a man available? Yes, Brutus.

Cassius contacts Brutus. He finds Brutus worrying about Caesar's growing power. Brutus said, upon hearing the people shouting:

> *I do fear, the people*
> *Choose Caesar for their king.*

Then says Cassius:

> *You would not have it so.*[2]

Brutus tells Cassius how he values honor and has no fear of death. Then Cassius, as if he had just read, *How to Win*

Friends and Influence People, starts to work on Brutus. He compliments him highly. He works on motives that make people buy. He shows Brutus how the people of Rome may "profit," how Brutus may profit. He appeals to Brutus' "pride." He sounds the note of Brutus' "affection" for home. He expresses "fear" that Brutus and himself will find dishonorable graves, if Caesar lives. He then takes a final fling, by working on the ego of Brutus, and gets Brutus interested enough to make a later appointment.

Then came the "follow-up" letters. Notes were thrown over the garden wall to Brutus. Notes were also thrown in the window.

As Cassius says:

> *For who so firm that cannot be seduced?*
> *. . . . . I will this night,*
> *In several hands, in at his windows throw,*
> *As if they came from several citizens,*
> *Writings, all tending to the great opinion*
> *That Rome holds of his name.*[3]

Follow-up letters.
Then another personal interview.
And Brutus is sold and joins the conspiracy.

Then the assassination takes place. Caesar is dead. During the assassination, one man, a very important man, left hurriedly. Maybe it reminded him of something. Maybe his wife wanted him at home to do some chores. Maybe he was scared. Who knows? He left. His name was Mark Antony. Later we shall hear more from him. But first he takes out a life insurance policy with disability benefits— the first one ever written. This is how it was done:

Mark sends a servant to Brutus, asking, "safe conduct."

He wanted an agreement from Brutus that he would not be killed or injured if he calls on Brutus. And Brutus underwrote that policy for Mark Antony by agreeing not to harm him in any way.

Now Mark appears in the Forum with a flourish and great courage. He can afford to be brave. He pays a tribute to the dead body of Caesar and then turning to the conspirators says:

> *I do beseech ye, if you bear me hard,*
> *Now, whilst your purpled hands do reek and smoke,*
> *Fulfil your pleasure.*[4]

Of course, Mark knew they would not hit him. He had that insurance policy in his pocket. He came to make a sale. In fact, his object was to make two sales in one interview. He wanted to sell Brutus the idea of allowing him to take Caesar's body to the market place and deliver a funeral oration.

Again Brutus was sold to his own undoing.

Antony sold Brutus, as Cassius had, because Brutus was an idealistic unsuspecting character.

But, Mark didn't sell Cassius, who was of an entirely different nature.

Remember what Cassius said when Mark Antony made this request of Brutus, and Brutus said:

> *You shall, Mark Antony.*[5]

Well, Cassius said:

> *Do not consent*
> *That Antony speak in his funeral:*
> *Know you how much the people may be moved*
> *By that which he will utter?*[6]

I've always had a feeling that Cassius was either a banker or a credit man. You can't use the hurry-up emotional method to sell a banker or a credit man. It just won't work. I know because I've tried it. I've rushed into my bank, and said, "Here's a note for $400. Please discount it and then place it to my credit. I'm catching the 4 o'clock plane."

And the answer invariably is: "No hurry, see us when you come back, and we'll make a decision."

They would not be rushed off their feet.

After all, a salesman should have some general idea of the type and temperament of his prospects, and the proper line of approach.

But, Antony did not have to sell Cassius. His prospect was Brutus. And Brutus was an egotistical, emotional salesman. And he reacted unfavorably to Cassius' objections. Brutus said in effect: "I'll make the first sales talk and that will be all there is to it. I don't care who follows me."

Many a modern salesman makes that mistake. It isn't necessarily the first or the second interview. It's the one that gets the order that counts.

But Brutus was an egotist. He had a reputation as a wonderful sales speaker. He felt sure that he would do the job so well that there would be no question about the results. Besides Brutus was a very honorable man—very lofty in character, and he, therefore, wanted it to appear that nothing was done to interfere with the other side presenting its story.

He also had an agreement from Antony that he was to speak on the virtues of Caesar and was not in any way to criticize the conspirators or stir up any feeling against them.

I want to call your attention to the way Brutus made this speech. He had the respect and admiration of the people of Rome. He was sincere in his purpose. He had no selfish thoughts, but only thought of the good of Rome. He was thrice "armed," as Shakespeare says, because he thought his cause was just. And yet, Shakespeare has him effectively use the fundamental principles of salesmanship.

THE LAWS OF A SALE

To sell myself I can be well contented,
So thou wilt buy, and pay, and use good dealing.[1]

The four fundamental laws of a sale are:
  (1) Get attention;
  (2) Create interest;
  (3) Arouse desire;
  (4) Force action.
There are many ways of getting attention, and that is the first law of a sale.

Without attention all effort is wasted.

An Arab guide, by waving a flag in front of his client's eyes, stops the client's thinking and then gets his attention.

The assassination of Caesar had not only obtained for Brutus the attention of the Roman people, it had aroused their interest as well. The red flag of murder had stopped momentarily the thinking of the Roman people, and Brutus not only obtained attention but undivided attention because his audience was both excited and curious. Brutus' opening statement is a masterpiece of selling.

Hear me for my cause, and be silent, that you may hear: believe me for mine honour, and have respect to mine honour, that you may believe: censure me in your wisdom, and awake your senses, that you may the better judge. If there be any in this assembly, any dear friend of Caesar's, to him I say that Brutus' love to Caesar was no less than his. If then that friend demand why Brutus rose against Caesar, this is my answer: not that I loved Caesar less, but that I loved Rome more.[2]

Brutus now has his audience on his side. He must now create desire, the third law of a sale.

Shakespeare, with his superior knowledge of the art of selling, has Brutus use an affirmative approach. In this way confidence is established, desire created, and action obtained. He refused to follow the slipshod methods of many of our modern salesmen—those who persist in using the negative approach. How many of these so-called salesmen not only lose business but actually close the door to any possibility of making a sale? They walk into an office, greet the prospect and say:

"Don't want to buy anything this morning, do you?"

"No. How did you happen to guess?"

"You wouldn't be interested in a new book, would you?"

"Certainly not," replies the prospect in the same negative vane.

"I couldn't interest you in a vacuum cleaner, could I?"

"You could not," would be the natural answer.

"You don't want to buy a new refrigerator, do you?"

"I do not," the prospect would answer.

Or, "I'm just one of those life insurance pests, and I came around to bother you a little this morning. You're not interested, are you?"

"You're right. I'm not."

No, Brutus did not say to his countrymen: "You don't think I should have killed Caesar, do you?"

Or, "Do you think we will be any better off now that I have killed Caesar?"

No. Brutus approached the matter with a very definite positive approach. He set up a standard of measurement. He asked them questions that they could only answer in his favor.

For example:

> *Had you rather Caesar were living, and*
> *die all slaves, than that Caesar were dead,*
> *to live all freemen?*[3]

Now how could you answer a question like that, if somebody asked it? Well, that's the way they answered it.

> *Who is here so base that would be a bond-*
> *man? If any, speak; for him have I offended.*[4]

Now who got up on that? You wouldn't have. Well, no one did. That's all there was to that.

> *Who is here so rude that would not be a Ro-*
> *man? If any, speak; for him have I offended.*[5]

No one would dare to stand up and say: "I would not be a Roman."

> *Who is here so vile that will not love his coun-*
> *try? If any, speak; for him have I offended.*[6]

And the crowd answered:

None, Brutus, none.[7]

Brutus replied:

Then none have I offended.[8]

And the sale was made.

You can't answer any of these questions asked by Brutus except in Brutus' favor. And that is the way the crowd answered them.

Brutus had set up a standard of measurement, and he had committed them to it. He had given them a choice, but it was a choice that could only be made in his favor.

If a modern drug store salesman says to you when you order a malted milk, "Will you have one or two eggs in it?" you can only answer easily by accepting one of the two propositions. In either case a sale was made. You bought either one or two eggs. If you are going to refuse, it takes more effort on your part, and, as many buyers are lazy, they "yield to weakness."

In other words, intelligent salesmanship makes it easy for the prospect to decide in your favor.

Or, if an insurance agent says to you: "Would you want this policy payable to your estate or to your widow?" he makes it difficult for you to answer it in any way except in his favor.

But Brutus, clever as he was in getting attention and immediately bridging over to the island of selfish interest of his audience, then creating desire by getting agreement and making them want to go along with him to accomplish a definite purpose, made a fatal error which is often made by a modern salesman. He did not properly use the fourth law of a sale.

He didn't close the deal.

He didn't get action.

He even did worse than that. He invited them to listen to his competitor, Mark Antony.

> *Let me depart alone,*
> *And, for my sake, stay here with Antony:*
> *Do grace to Caesar's corpse, and grace his speech*
> *Tending to Caesar's glories, which Mark Antony*
> *By our permission is allow'd to make.*
> *I do entreat you, not a man depart.*[9]

It was as if he had said: "Don't act on my proposition now, take it home and think it over. Listen to my competitor tell his side of it. After all, I may be wrong."

Brutus was so sure that his cause was just that he felt this was a safe procedure. But, many a salesman who has a better proposition loses the business to a more vigorous salesman with a much poorer proposition.

Brutus forgot, as we say in the automobile business, to get the down payment.

He didn't get action. He didn't get action at the psychological moment, the moment when the crowd was with him and perfectly willing to do whatever he told it to do. He didn't close the sale.

He forgot, as Dick Borden puts it, his "so what." Or rather, he chose a very bad "so what" by advising the people to listen to Mark Antony.

Of course, there are prospects who would prefer Brutus' method of closing. They prefer not to be motivated. They prefer to take the matter under advisement. They prefer to hear all sides. To visit competitors and make comparisons, then make their decisions "away from the glamour and personality of the salesman."

Shakespeare knew this and being a master salesman he presents through Brutus this method of selling.

Dr. C. E. Albright, of Milwaukee, a representative of the Northwestern Mutual Life Insurance Company, has used with striking success the Shakespeare-Brutus method. But this plan of selling only works with a small minority, and mobs or crowds are not minorities and react like the majority of people would react. The majority of prospects must receive emotional motivation.

My theory of salesmanship is that the salesman seldom loses by giving a man a chance to pay him when the man is in the humor to pay—to get the settlement at the time it is easiest to get it—in other words, as the saying goes in the life insurance field, to get cash with the application.

An old planter down in the South, retired from his job and opened a little general merchandising store to sell supplies to the colored tenants. He sold these supplies on credit and expected to receive his payment when the cotton was picked. One day a little negro named Mose came in and said: "Mars John, Ah got three bales. Ah figguh as how Ah owes you all about two ob dem. Would you all mind givin' me the cash fo da diffunce?"

"Certainly, Mose," said Mars John, and he did.

Mose took the cash and went across the street to a cash store that was only open during the season and bought a brand new outfit for himself, hat, suit, shoes, new shirt, flaming red tie, and a big cigar. He came back to Mars John's store and sat down and started to smoke.

Mars John noticed him and said: "Mose, where did you get all that finery?"

"Why, Ah went across the street to da cash store and bought it," said Mose innocently. Mars John became excited, and his temper flared.

"Why, you black scoundrel! Do you mean to tell me that after I've been giving you credit all these years, you took that money I just gave you and went across the street and spent it with my competitor? Why didn't you spend that cash here with me?"

Mose's eyes stuck out like knots on a log. " 'Fore God, Mars John," Mose replied. "Ah didn't know you all sold for cash."

Why not improve the methods that Shakespeare has Brutus use in closing by simply saying: "Do you want to give me a check, or do you prefer paying cash?" or, "Shall I make out a check for you, or would you rather give me your own personal check?" or some such statement that only permits an answer in your favor? Then you will learn one of the best lessons in salesmanship taught years ago by Shakespeare.

I think possibly there was a reason for Shakespeare's calling attention to Brutus' weakness in this particular sale, because he now is going to present to you a character through whom he can use all of the technique of a finished salesman. Let us now present Mark Antony, the puppet Shakespeare created to give to you the finest exhibition of salesmanship ever recorded.

Shakespeare realized what Mark Antony is up against. He isn't approaching a prospect who is friendly and interested. He is approaching a rather hostile audience, and his first job is to get the attention of the audience.

They didn't kill a ruler every day in Rome, so this was an unusual event. There had been tremendous emotional excitement. Brutus had made a sales presentation, and the audience was sold on not only the fact that Brutus was a very honorable man, but that Brutus was right in what he did and in what he advocated.

The members of the audience had probably made a lot of extemporaneous speeches themselves. They were tired and restless and didn't want to hear any more speeches. Into this howling emotional mob came Mark Antony bearing the dead body of Caesar. In this act he excited the curiosity of the crowd. But that act alone would not calm the excited mob.

He had to face the fact that he must use the four laws of a sale, the first of which is to get attention.

You remember how he struggled to get attention. *Friends, Romans, countrymen, lend me your ears,*[10] he shouted. But, he didn't get their attention.

I've always felt sorry for Mark. I went over to Italy several years ago and looked at the place where Mark made that speech. I can visualize the crowd milling around, talking, excited, and antagonistic.

My mind went back to an experience I had when I went on a trade trip for the Chamber of Commerce at Kansas City, Missouri. It was a good many years ago, and we had a marvelous band. Every time we would stop at some small town, the band would play a selection to see if we couldn't get some of the crowd to come to the platform. The crowd would gather around the rear end of the train. The band would stop, and then I would hop up on the platform and make a speech. Then the band would have to play another selection to see if we couldn't get some of the crowd to come back.

Mark Antony didn't have any band. If he had had a band, it would have been a great help.

But, a serious situation like that would not stump

Shakespeare. Shakespeare has Mark Antony say as an attention getter, this:

I come to bury Caesar.[11]

There is a hush, and the crowd said: "Good, let Mark bury Caesar." Somebody had to do it. Everybody was in favor of having Caesar buried. There was no argument about that. It seemed the proper thing to do.

But, having gotten the attention of the crowd, and before they could get their minds away from the idea of burying Caesar, Mark Antony gave them something else to think about.

I remember one day when sitting in my office in Norfolk, Virginia, a gentleman named Van Noppen came into the outer office, spoke to my secretary, and said: "Could I see Mr. Burruss for three minutes on a matter of vital importance to him?"

I got up and came to the door, my mind still on the note that the bank had advised me was now due. I was wondering whether it would be renewed without a curtail. This was of great importance to me. My mind was fully occupied with that thought. (I had also learned over the years that I had spent as a salesman this fact: only one thought can occupy the mind at a time. And there was no room in the mind unless that thought was ejected.)

Well, the first thing Mr. Van Noppen did was to eject that thought.

How?

By grabbing my hand and saying: "My name is Van Noppen, V-A-N N-O-P-P-E-N. Van Noppen. It's Dutch." Then he twisted my hand. My mind instantly left the note and went to my hand.

Before it got back to the note I owned a history of
North Carolina. He had used the same technique William
Shakespeare developed for Mark Antony, who got the
crowd's attention and then immediately bridged over to
their island of selfish interest by saying:

> *He hath brought many captives home to Rome,*
> *Whose ransoms did the general coffers fill.*[12]

Now what did Mark Antony mean by that statement?
What does it mean to us?
What did it mean to them?
We know that as a ransom getter and a tribute levier,
Caesar had the world skinned. He was the original kid-
napper.
He captured prominent people and held them for ran-
som. He conquered tribes and levied tributes upon them.
Now all of this money went into the general coffers.
General coffers translated into our language mean the
treasury. We also know that the money in the treasury all
went out to pay the costs of running the government in
Rome; Caesar did not take any of it.
We know that, and they knew it. But the thing that
they knew, which most of us do not know, unless we happen to be a student of taxation in the Roman era, is this:
no Roman citizen paid any taxes whatsoever during
Caesar's regime, and when Mark Antony said to them:
"He hath brought many captives home to Rome," that
translated into our language before a crowd in this country at this time would have been a statement something
like this: "Boys, Caesar has been paying all the taxes.
Who is going to pay them now?"
That would interest us immediately.

We would want to know how much we were going to have to pay, and how.

And it interested them, because they, too, even in that day, recognized the fact that it's nicer not to have to pay taxes than to pay them. And so Mark Antony immediately got their interest.

When he got their interest, he immediately gave them a reason for action.

Probably over 90 per cent of sales are made by an appeal to emotions after you have given a reason.

Mark Antony had a very definite job in mind. He had to build up the fact that there was nothing in Caesar's life or his actions that could in any way justify the conspirators in their act of killing him.

But, he had to tread softly, for the crowd knew that Mark Antony only spoke because of the fact that Brutus had given him permission and he was therefore under obligation to Brutus to talk only about Caesar and his greatness. He had agreed to say nothing uncomplimentary about the conspirators.

Having taken the first two steps of the sale, getting attention and creating desire, Shakespeare now has Mark Antony attempt to create desire. In this particular case Mark Antony's object is to rebuild the fires of affection that the people had for Caesar, to rebuild the confidence they had in him, to renew the respect they had for his fairness and justice.

He also must very subtly destroy the confidence of the people in the conspirators who killed Caesar. This requires the master touch. A man would have to be a super-salesman to do all these things—and that is just what Shakespeare was! That is why he could tell Mark Antony what to say and do. Let us see how he does it.

BUYING MOTIVES

Set thy person forth to sell.[1]

Shakespeare has Mark Antony sell the Romans by adroit appeal to their "buying motives."

In this way only could he create desire strong enough to persuade them to do the things he wanted them to do.

> He wanted the people to lose their faith in the conspirators.
> He wanted the people to turn against the conspirators with fury and drive them out of Rome.
> He wanted them to raise an army for him.
> He wanted them to make him ruler of Rome.
> He has taken the first two steps of a sale.
> He got attention.
> He created interest, and now to
> Arouse desire.

To do this he has worked upon their desire for profit and has shown them how they "profited" under Caesar.

His reference to the fact that Caesar conquered tribes and brought captives home to Rome who were held for ransom immediately touched the "profit motive."

He then appeals to their "sense of reason" and now makes an appeal to stir up their "affection" for Caesar.

> *When that the poor have cried, Caesar hath wept:*
> *Ambition should be made of sterner stuff:*
> *Yet Brutus says he was ambitious;*

And Brutus is an honourable man.

. . . .

I speak not to disprove what Brutus spoke,
But here I am to speak what I do know.
You all did love him once, not without cause:
What cause withholds you then to mourn for him?
O judgement! thou art fled to brutish beasts,
And men have lost their reason. Bear with me;
My heart is in the coffin there with Caesar,
And I must pause till it come back to me.[2]

Oh, that only more modern salesmen would sometimes *pause* and let the prospect say something.

We would have a whole lot *more* sales and a whole lot *less* conversation. But the average salesman says: "I have come here to make a speech, and, by gosh, I am going to make it whether I sell anything or not."

This, of course, is very poor technique. It isn't important what is going on in the salesman's mind, but it is vital for a salesman to know what is going on in the mind of the prospect. And good technique demands that we do everything possible to find out not only what is going on in the mind of the prospect, but what his reactions are.

We get our sales not by talking, but by listening and giving the other fellow a chance to say something.

Mark Antony listened and the crowd said:

Methinks there is much reason in his sayings.

If thou consider rightly of the matter
Caesar has had great wrong.

                      Has he, masters?
I fear there will a worse come in his place.

There's not a nobler man in Rome than Antony.[3]

Now, Mark knows what is in his crowd's mind. That is the way to make selling easier. First find out what is in the mind of the prospect. It is not important about what the salesman is thinking. The only important thing is: what is the buyer thinking? And when you find that out you find the answer to your problem. The way to discover that is to let him say something, but most salesmen do not give the prospect a chance.

Now Mark Antony touches three buying motives. He appeals to their "pride" and he also appeals to their "curiosity," and again touches upon the "profit" motive.

In his first sentence he calls attention to the fact that Caesar, probably the most outstanding man in all the world, was a Roman, a home town boy. That was an appeal to their "pride."

And then in producing the will he naturally creates "curiosity." But let us see for ourselves just how Shakespeare has Mark Antony conduct this part of the sale.

> But yesterday the word of Caesar might
> Have stood against the world: now lies he there,
> And none so poor to do him reverence.
> O masters, if I were disposed to stir
> Your hearts and minds to mutiny and rage,
> I should do Brutus wrong and Cassius wrong,
> Who, you all know, are honourable men:
> I will not do them wrong; I rather choose
> To wrong the dead, to wrong myself and you,
> Than I will wrong such honourable men.
> But here's a parchment with the seal of Caesar;
> I found it in his closet; 'tis his will:
> But let the commons hear this testament—
> Which, pardon me, I do not mean to read—
> And they would go and kiss dead Caesar's wounds
> And dip their napkins in his sacred blood,

> *Yea, beg a hair of him for memory,*
> *And, dying, mention it within their wills,*
> *Bequeathing, it as a rich legacy*
> *Unto their issue.*[4]

Why do you suppose they would have felt that way about it? Naturally, each one in the crowd thinks: "There must be something in that will for me." And he wants to know what it is. So the people say:

> *We'll hear the will; read it, Mark Antony.*
>
> *The will, the will! we will hear Caesar's will.*[5]

He replied:

> *Have patience, gentle friends, I must not read it;*
> *It is not meet you know how Caesar loved you.*
> *You are not wood, you are not stones, but men;*
> *And, being men, hearing the will of Caesar,*
> *It will inflame you, it will make you mad.*

And then he said aside, but so that all of the crowd could hear him:

> *'Tis good you know not that you are his heirs;*
> *For if you should, O, what would come of it!*[6]

Naturally, that did not still their curiosity. The profit motive appeal has been very cleverly applied. They now know they are Caesar's heirs. The next question is: "How much?" That is what they want to know now.

They shouted:

> *Read the will; we'll hear it, Antony;*
> *You shall read us the will, Caesar's will.*[7]

Antony said:

> *Will you be patient? will you stay awhile?*
> *I have o'ershot myself to tell you of it:*
> *I fear I wrong the honourable men*
> *Whose daggers have stabb'd Caesar; I do fear it.*[8]

Remember Mark Antony had agreed not to say anything uncomplimentary about the conspirators. See how cleverly Shakespeare, by the preceding statements of Mark Antony, makes the crowd shout disapproval of the conspirators. Let us see what the crowd said:

> *They were traitors:*

And with a very sneering emphasis, quoted Antony:

> *Honourable men!*
>
> *The will! the testament!*
>
> *They were villains, murderers: the will!*
> *read the will.*[9]

The crowd knows that they are beneficiaries under Caesar's will. They now want to know how much, so they are very impatient to have Mark read the will. And Mark continues:

> *You will compel me then to read the will?*
> *Then make a ring about the corpse of Caesar,*
> *And let me show you him that made the will.*
> *Shall I descend? and will you give me leave?*[10]
>
> *Come down.*
>
> *Descend.*
>
> *You shall have leave.*
>
> *Room for Antony, most noble Antony.*[11]

Now Antony, as a salesman, is in the driver's seat. When he was trying to get their attention, the crowd controlled the situation. Now the crowd wanted him to tell the story, and he controlled the situation. This is of great importance to a salesman.

It means a lot to you, as a salesman, to have the prospect say to you in effect:

"Come in, have a seat. I'm very much interested in your proposition. Tell me all about it."

But he only does that when he thinks you have something for him that he wants. How different is it when the salesman encounters the buyer who has that "I manufacture my own ice" look in his eye, and says with a haughty manner: "What can I do for you?" This is the type of situation that demands the salesman reply in his most dignified way: "You can't do a thing for me, but I can do an awful lot for you."

But, when you have reached the point where the buyer is anxious to have you talk to him, then I repeat: you are in the driver's seat. You have the whip hand position. You are the man who is doing the buyer a favor.

The crowd is still crying for the will.

Mark comes down. Does he read the will?

Would you?

What is the idea he wanted to sell them?

That the men who killed Caesar were not public spirited; that they killed Caesar because of personal grievance, jealousy, and ingratitude. He had to sell them that thought. And he must never forget his real objective is to sell the crowd that Brutus, whom they loved and respected most, was the worst traitor of the lot. So, instead of picking up the will and reading it, he comes down and picks up the mantle off the dead body of Caesar and says:

You all do know this mantle: I remember
The first time ever Caesar put it on;
'Twas on a summer's evening, in his tent,
That day he overcome the Nervii.

Again appealing to the buying motive, "pride."

Look, in this place ran Cassius' dagger through:
See what a rent the envious Casca made:
Through this the well-beloved Brutus stabb'd;
And as he pluck'd his cursed steel away,
Mark how the blood of Caesar follow'd it,
As rushing out of doors, to be resolved
If Brutus so unkindly knock'd, or no:
For Brutus, as you know, was Caesar's angel:
Judge, O you gods, how dearly Caesar loved him!
This was the most unkindest cut of all;
For when the noble Caesar saw him stab,
Ingratitude, more strong than traitors' arms,
Quite vanquish'd him: then burst his mighty heart;

A very effective appeal to the well-known buying motive, "affection."

O, now you weep, and, I perceive you feel
The dint of pity: these are gracious drops.
Kind souls, what weep you when you but behold
Our Caesar's vesture wounded? Look you here,
Here is himself, marr'd, as you see, with traitors.[12]

Well, the crowd rose up on its hind legs and started out to do what you would have done under the same circumstances. They started out to clean up the gang, and Mark Antony called them back. He did not want them to go away without being thoroughly sold. He didn't want them to start an attack on the conspirators until they knew why they were doing it and how it would profit them.

He had pointed out to them, through the profit motive, that Caesar had paid their taxes, that he had left them a mention in his will.

But, he had not told them what was in the will, and he knew that if they stopped to think they might ask themselves the question:

"Why should we do this? I didn't see the will."

He calls them back to finish the sale by saying:

> *They that have done this deed are honourable;*
> *What private griefs they have, alas, I know not,*
> *That made them do it; they are wise and honourable,*
> *And will, no doubt, with reasons answer you.*[13]

Now this is dirty selling, because Mark Antony was a dirty salesman. But Shakespeare pointed out time and again that dirty selling doesn't pay, that like a boomerang it comes back and strikes you, making you very sick in your stomach.

Oh, yes, Mark Antony was a dirty salesman and he failed, as all dirty salesmen will fail in the end.

He had made it impossible for Brutus to answer him. He had shut out competition. The crowd started to leave and Mark Antony again called to them to come back.

> *Why, friends, you go to do you know not what:*
> *Wherein hath Caesar thus deserved your loves?*
> *Alas, you know not; I must tell you, then.*[14]

And he produced the will and read the will to them. He showed them that Caesar living had paid all their taxes

and Caesar dead had left them all his property. Could anything be fairer than that? And then he said:

> *I am no orator, as Brutus is;*
> *But, as you know me all, a plain blunt man,*
> *That love my friend; and that they know full well*
> *. . . . .*
> *For I have neither wit, nor words, nor worth,*
> *Action, nor utterance, not the power of speech,*
> *To stir men's blood: I only speak right on;*
> *I tell you that which you yourselves do know;*
> *Show you sweet Caesar's wounds, poor poor dumb mouths,*
> *And bid them speak for me; but were I Brutus,*
> *And Brutus Antony, there were an Antony*
> *Would ruffle up your spirits, and put a tongue*
> *In every wound of Caesar, that should move*
> *The stones of Rome to rise and mutiny.*[15]

Here the fourth law of a sale, getting action, is brought
out very clearly. And Shakespeare also uses the very
clever technique in having Antony deny that he was a
real salesman, but rather just a layman, and that he didn't
have any ability to sway them. That he only told them
what they themselves did know.

He worked up the crowd to a frenzy. They had yielded
to the buying motives, the last of which is "yielding to
weakness."

Their calm, sober judgment had given away to emotional reactions and they went out to do a job.

Shakespeare, through Mark Antony, got action.

You know what the Romans did.

They drove the conspirators out of Rome.

They killed a lot of fellows who had the same names,
but were in no way connected with the conspirators. The
mob just did not like their names.

They raised an army for Mark Antony, and he would
have been the greatest man in Rome but for one thing.

What was that one thing?

Let us tell you in the next chapter.

SINCERITY

> *I must prevent thee, Cimber.*
> *These couchings and these lowly courtesies*
> *Might fire the blood of ordinary men,*
> *And turn pre-ordinance and first decree*
> *Into the law of children. Be not fond,*
> *To think that Caesar bears such rebel blood*
> *That will be thaw'd from the true quality*
> *With that which melteth fools, I mean, sweet words,*
> *Low-crooked court'sies and base spaniel-fawning.*[1]

The one thing that Mark Antony lacked for total success was sincerity. Indeed, Shakespeare proves over and
over again the folly of insincerity and the value of sincerity.

In using the word "sincerity," I mean it in the com-
monly accepted sense: To be sincere in expression means
to be honest, fair, and truthful.

Shakespeare defines true sincerity when he has Julia
say of Proteus:

> *His words are bonds, his oaths are oracles;*
> *His love sincere, his thoughts immaculate;*
> *His tears pure messengers sent from his heart;*
> *His heart as far from fraud as heaven from earth.*[2]

No organization can last without sincerity.

No institution can endure without it.

No individual can succeed without it.

No salesman worthy of the name would want to sell without it.

That one thing—sincerity—we must possess or we must eventually fail as Mark Antony did. Macbeth, Iago, King Richard III, and Cardinal Wolsey all failed because all were insincere. Caesar, although assassinated, still commands respect in history as a great and just ruler of his people, because of his sincerity. Hamlet and Horatio also give an excellent example of what Shakespeare meant by sincere friendship and understanding.

It is, of course, important to get along with other human beings. It is important to win their respect, confidence, and admiration; but, it is far more important to keep your own self-respect. And you cannot do that if you are not sincere.

Our word "sincerity" comes from two Latin words— *sine cera*—literally meaning "without wax."

It seems that in the Roman days certain sculptors covered up their errors or carelessness, or the fact that they had selected a poor piece of material, by the use of wax. Instead of throwing away the piece of marble that had cracks or defects, these sculptors merely filled in the cracks with wax, polished it up with marble dust and sold the piece without telling the customers. Later when the wax dried out, it fell out of the cracks and caused the customers to become resentful.

At that time they may or may not have had "Better Business Bureaus" to check upon merchants' business methods, but they did have a certain amount of honesty and common sense. So the better and more ethical sculptors got together and advertised their works of art as *sine cera* without wax. The doctrine of *caveat emptor*— let the buyer beware, or "we guarantee nothing" or "as is" —was replaced by a simple policy of "satisfaction guaranteed," or let us say, "sincerity in selling."

Since that time we have had many sincere salesmen, salesmen who neither actually misrepresent the facts nor by clever concealment create a wrong impression. True, we have some who consider any method or plan that gets the business perfectly all right, and, unfortunately, we have too many who skirt dangerously near the precipice of outright insincerity.

How many of us have seen a sign in a shop window that says:

BARGAIN $5.00
(DOWN)

In a remote corner of the card is the word "down" in letters so small that we can hardly read them. Many of us have heard salesmen who have been deliberately taught to trick the public by the following method:

When the customer asks the price of the article, the salesman replies, "Mrs. Jones, I know you will be pleased to know that you can have this wonderful gadget for only $5.00 (the voice rising perceptibly on the word, '$5.00')" and then dropping the voice to almost a whisper and trailing off into space, the salesman adds, "and $3.00 a month for twenty-four months."

But the really honest salesman accepts *this* definition of sincere salesmanship: *An honest sale is a sale where both the buyer and the seller profit.* If the buyer profits and the seller loses, it is a rebate. If the seller profits and the buyer loses, it is a filmflam. There was too much "wax."

Sincerity in selling today demands of the salesman this simple code of ethics:

(1) Find out the buyer's problem.

(2) Help him to solve it.

If, in the solving of the buyer's problem, your services or your products are needed, then you will have rendered him a real service or profit and will yourself have made a profit.

This is especially true under the national emergency that now confronts us. We are working under a war economy, and it can make or break salesmen everywhere. Due to rulings by the Priority Board of the Office of Production Management, many manufacturers have had to curtail production. Salesmen representing these manufacturers or their sales outlets in contacting customers are sometimes inclined to make the serious mistake of condemning our government for this curtailment.

While it may be true that our government may make mistakes and at times be unjust to certain groups, the salesmen should recognize this fact: to help destroy loyalty to our government when it is bending every effort to be prepared to defend private enterprise and to be able to continue to guarantee to us the right of selecting our own vocation and place of work is to help destroy the foundations of our business system. To do this is not in keeping with sincere patriotism.

While not perfect, the free enterprise system has in 165 years in this country outstripped all other plans of operations from the standpoint of the greatest development of opportunity for all citizens to obtain for themselves the better things of life.

A salesman may think it advantageous, in order to prevent customers from blaming him or his house, to turn their wrath on the government. Suppose such salesmen succeed to the extent that our program for defense crumbles and we fall under the "New Order," as so many countries in Europe have.

Ask some of our manufacturers who have tried to do business with Hitler whether they prefer our system or his. His plan is founded on insincerity and relies for its strength and success on chicanery and fraud.

Here, when we sell a carload of implements, for instance, we get money that is good for face value, and we can use it to buy what we want. However, if we ship our goods across the Atlantic to Germany with the understanding and promise that we will receive compensation in bills of exchange, good for face value in our own money, we are apt to find ourselves fleeced.

Adolph Hitler, the most outstanding exponent and advocate of insincerity in the world, today, has so manipulated things that we have to take for our merchandise, when in German docks or warehouses whatever he wants to give us, perhaps 5,000 canary birds, 10,000 tulip bulbs, 15,000 razor blades, or what-have-you—and pay an additional booty beside, instead of getting what we were promised.

It has been said that Adolph Hitler's colossal egotism has led him to believe he can avoid the mistakes of the late Kaiser Wilhelm, Napoleon, and other great war lords and succeed where they failed—that he can be the first to make insincerity and fraud triumph.

The sort of ethics Hitler has espoused involving hypocrisy, cajolery, murder, disguised by a pretense of sincerity, was aptly illustrated by Shakespeare in the play depicting Richard III. In this, Richard apparently won love and loyalty through clever pretense of friendship and insincere promises. He then struck down all who got in his way, whether wife, brother, relative, friend, or foe, and he got the kingship and the power he sought. But, finally, he lost everything, including his life. Shakespeare records him as an insincere monster.

Hitler's egotism may make him feel that he can succeed where Richard III failed, by being more insincere and ruthless on a far grander scale. He may feel that he can glorify insincerity and prove that sincerity does not pay. Time alone will tell.

But the purpose of our country and other democracies and lovers of freedom and decency is to defeat Hitler and establish sincerity as a world policy. Credit among nations is built on sincerity, and we have to have credit to maintain business and social relations successfully.

So it all adds up to this: we cannot get along without sincerity.

Sincerity is not a cloak to be thrown over our shoulders to conceal hypocrisy and double-dealing. Not what we appear to be, but what we really are is the thing that counts. The test of the value of sincerity lies not in the apparent gains we make or lose by being sincere. Sincerity cannot be measured in dollars and cents, or in the acquisition of power, but in what it does for our character and future. After all, we have to live with ourselves, and it is worth a lot to have mind and conscience at peace.

In too many instances in the press, on the radio, in published books and articles, and in platform addresses, writters and speakers advocate methods of selling merchandise or of making friends or gaining influence that are far from sincere. These may prove profitable for a time, but in the long run will assist in destroying the public's confidence in the sincerity of all of us.

Insincerity can only be profitable occasionally in a financial sense when used skilfully by the few to fool the many. Sooner or later no one is fooled, and no financial profit ensues.

The apparent Nazi success of a policy of insincerity may have been made easier by the prevalent attitude of peoples everywhere in the past generation. Expressed pungently, it is: "What's in it for me?"

Only a greedy and somewhat dishonest person can be sold a gold brick. He thinks he is out-slicking the slicker. Only a stupid egotist can hope to go through life unchecked in a career of lying and insincere statement.

When a greater measure of idealism returns—and return it will—we will have a different standard of measurement. Possibly the youth of tomorrow, instead of asking, "What's in it for me?" may ask a question that will help to move the human race forward, will help to put its thinking on a higher plane, will help to put human and business relations on a real basis of sincerity.

The question asked then may well be: "What effect will my action have upon my character and peace of mind and upon others?"

Shakespeare has given us countless examples of the folly of insincerity. The pages of his works are full of expressions of sincere loyalty and sincere affection. Hamlet's love for Horatio was sincere and caused him, while dying, to say to Horatio who wanted to die with Hamlet and tried to drink from the poisoned cup:

> *As thou 'rt a man,*
> *Give me the cup: . . . .*
> *O good Horatio, what a wounded name,*
> *Things standing thus unknown, shall live behind me!*

> *Absent thee from felicity a while,*
> *And in this harsh world draw thy breath in pain,*
> *To tell my story.*[3]

Horatio, according to Shakespeare, gave up an easy way out of life and faced a cruel fortune because of his sincerity and loyalty to his friend.

Is it too much to ask of salesmen to be sincere? Is it too much to ask them in facing today's problems to remember that the world needs men who have the courage of some of the characters glorified by Shakespeare?

Horatio lived for sincerity's sake.

Caesar died for it!

And although Brutus engaged in an unworthy project, he did it only because of his sincere belief that he was serving his country. And Shakespeare has Antony say of him:

> *This was the noblest Roman of them all:*
> *All the conspirators, save only he,*
> *Did that they did in envy of great Caesar;*
> *He only, in a general honest thought*
> *And common good to all, made one of them.*
> *His life was gentle, and the elements*
> *So mix'd in him that Nature might stand up*
> *And say to all the world, "This was a man!"*[4]

Footnotes

FOOTNOTES

FOR the reader who is interested in looking up quotations in this book, each quotation has been footnoted, and the references follow. Each chapter's footnotes are numbered beginning with 1. The author of all works mentioned below was William Shakespeare, unless otherwise indicated.

WORLD'S BEST SALESMAN

[1]There is a tide in the affairs of men—*The Tragedy of Julius Caesar*, Act IV, Scene iii.
[2]Opinion's but a fool, that makes us—*Pericles, Prince of Tyre*, Act II, Scene ii.

CONFIDENCE

[1]Our doubts are traitors—*Measure for Measure*, Act I, Scene iv.
[2]Our doubts are traitors—*Ibid.*
[3]Our doubts are traitors—*Ibid.*
[4]As gentle and as jocund as to jest—*The Tragedy of King Richard II*, Act I, Scene iii.

ENTHUSIASM—THE WILL TO WIN

[1]I see you stand like greyhounds—*The Life of King Henry V*, Act III, Scene i.
[2]I will attend her here—*The Taming of the Shrew*, Act II, Scene i.

[3]Once more unto the breach, dear friends—*The Life of King Henry V*, Act III, Scene i.

[4]There's a divinity that shapes our ends—*The Tragedy of Hamlet, Prince of Denmark*, Act V, Scene ii.

[5]The quality of mercy is not strain'd—*The Merchant of Venice*, Act IV, Scene i.

OPEN-MINDEDNESS

[1]O day and night, but this is wondrous strange!—*The Tragedy of Hamlet, Prince of Denmark*, Act I, Scene v.

[2]There is a tide in the affairs of men—*The Tragedy of Julius Caesar*, Act IV, Scene iii.

[3]To be, or not to be—*The Tragedy of Hamlet, Prince of Denmark*, Act III, Scene i.

HUMAN UNDERSTANDING

[1]The quality of mercy is not strain'd—*The Merchant of Venice*, Act IV, Scene i.

[2]The proper study of mankind is man—*Alexander Pope, An Essay on Man*, Epistle II, Line 1.

[3]Or that the Everlasting had not fix'd—*The Tragedy of Hamlet, Prince of Denmark*, Act I, Scene ii.

[4]To die, to sleep—*Ibid.*, Act III, Scene i.

[5]The undiscover'd country from whose bourn—*Ibid.*

[6]Canst thou not minister to a mind diseased—*The Tragedy of Macbeth*, Act V, Scene iii.

[7]There is nothing either good or bad—*The Tragedy of Hamlet, Prince of Denmark*, Act II, Scene ii.

[8]Sir, I love you more than words can wield the matter—*The Tragedy of King Lear*, Act I, Scene i.

[9]I am made of that self metal—*Ibid.*

[10]Good my lord—*Ibid.*

[11]He that loves to be flattered—*The Life of Timon of Athens,* Act I, Scene i.

[12]Good reasons must of force give place to better—*The Tragedy of Julius Caesar,* Act IV, Scene iii.

[13]Thus conscience doth make cowards of us all—*The Tragedy of Hamlet, Prince of Denmark,* Act III, Scene i.

[14]A thought which, quarter'd, hath but one part wisdom—*Ibid.,* Act IV, Scene iv.

[15]Neither a borrower nor a lender be—*Ibid.,* Act I, Scene iii.

AN ALL-OUT EFFORT FOR SUCCESS

[1]The fault, dear Brutus, is not in our stars—*The Tragedy of Julius Caesar,* Act I, Scene ii.

[2] . . . Duke of Gloucester stop the funeral procession—*The Tragedy of King Richard III,* Act I, Scene ii.

[3] . . . Cassius wins Brutus—*The Tragedy of Julius Caesar,* Act I, Scene ii.

[4] . . . Othello, the Moor, wins Desdemona . . .—*The Tragedy of Othello, The Moor of Venice,* Act I, Scene iii.

[5]That I may pour my spirits in thine ear—*The Tragedy of Macbeth,* Act I, Scene v.

[6] . . . full o' the milk of human kindness—*Ibid.*

[7]Ha! I like not that—*The Tragedy of Othello, The Moor of Venice,* Act III, Scene iii.

MAKING THE VOICE WORK FOR YOU

[1]Speak the speech . . . as I pronounced it to you—*The*

Tragedy of Hamlet, Prince of Denmark, Act III, Scene ii.

[2]Speak the speech, I pray you—*Ibid.*

[3]Nor do not saw the air too much with your hand—*Ibid.*

[4]Suit the action to the word—*Ibid.*

[5]Give every man thy ear—*Ibid.,* Act I, Scene iii.

[6]And let those that play your clowns—*Ibid.,* Act III, Scene ii.

[7]Gratiano speaks an infinite deal of nothing—*The Merchant of Venice,* Act I, Scene i.

GOOD ETHICS AND CODE OF PROCEDURE

[1]But he that filches from me my good name—*The Tragedy of Othello, The Moor of Venice,* Act III, Scene iii.

[2]Costly thy habit as thy purse can buy—*The Tragedy of Hamlet, Prince of Denmark,* Act I, Scene iii.

[3]Assume a virtue, if you have it not—*Ibid.,* Act III, Scene iv.

[4]Those friends thou hast—*Ibid.,* Act I, Scene iii.

[5]Give every man thy ear—*Ibid.*

[6]This above all: to thine own self be true—*Ibid.*

SALES TECHNIQUE

[1]All the world's a stage—*As You Like It,* Act II, Scene vii.

[2]I do fear, the people choose Caesar for their king—*The Tragedy of Julius Caesar,* Act I, Scene ii.

[3]For who so firm that cannot be seduced—*Ibid.*

[4]I do beseech ye, if you bear me hard—*Ibid.,* Act III, Scene i.

[5]You shall, Mark Antony—*Ibid.*
[6]Do not consent that Antony speak in his funeral—*Ibid.*

THE LAWS OF A SALE

[1]To sell myself I can be well contented—*"Venus and Adonis,"* Line 513-14.
[2]Hear me for my cause, and be silent—*The Tragedy of Julius Caesar,* Act III, Scene ii.
[3]Had you rather Caesar were living—*Ibid.*
[4]Who is here so base that would be a bondman—*Ibid.*
[5]Who is here so rude that would not be a Roman—*Ibid.*
[6]Who is here so vile that will not love his country—*Ibid.*
[7]None, Brutus, none—*Ibid.*
[8]Then none have I offended—*Ibid.*
[9]Let me depart alone—*Ibid.*
[10]Friends, Romans, countrymen, lend me your ears—*Ibid.*
[11]I come to bury Caesar—*Ibid.*
[12]He hath brought many captives home to Rome—*Ibid.*

BUYING MOTIVES

[1]Set thy person forth to sell—*"The Passionate Pilgrim,"* Line 409.
[2]When that the poor have cried, Caesar hath wept—*The Tragedy of Julius Caesar,* Act III, Scene ii.
[3]Methinks there is much reason in his sayings—*Ibid.*
[4]But yesterday the word of Caesar might
 Have stood against the world.—*Ibid.*
[5]We'll hear the will—*Ibid.*
[6]Have patience, gentle friends, I must not read it—*Ibid.*
[7]Read the will; we'll hear it, Antony—*Ibid.*
[8]Will you be patient? will you stay awhile—*Ibid.*

[9]They were traitors—*Ibid.*
[10]You will compel me then to read the will—*Ibid.*
[11]Come down—*Ibid.*
[12]You all do know this mantle—*Ibid.*
[13]They that have done this deed are honourable—*Ibid.*
[14]Why, friends, you go to do you know not what—*Ibid.*
[15]I am no orator, as Brutus is—*Ibid.*

SINCERITY

[1]I must prevent thee, Cimber—*The Tragedy of Julius Caesar,* Act III, Scene i.
[2]His words are bonds—*The Two Gentlemen of Verona,* Act II, Scene vii.
[3]As thou 'rt a man, give me the cup—*The Tragedy of Hamlet, Prince of Denmark,* Act V, Scene ii.
[4]This was the noblest Roman of them all—*The Tragedy of Julius Caesar,* Act V, Scene v.